# THE MODERN, THE POSTMODERN, AND THE FACT OF TRANSITION

*The Paradigm Shift through Peninsular Literatures*

**Robert Simon**

University Press of America,® Inc.
Lanham · Boulder · New York · Toronto · Plymouth, UK

**Copyright © 2012 by**
**University Press of America,® Inc.**
4501 Forbes Boulevard
Suite 200
Lanham, Maryland 20706
UPA Acquisitions Department (301) 459-3366

Estover Road
Plymouth PL6 7PY
United Kingdom

Library of Congress Control Number: 2011940494
ISBN: 978-0-7618-5764-8 (paperback : alk. paper)
eISBN: 978-0-7618-5765-5

⊖™ The paper used in this publication meets the minimum
requirements of American National Standard for Information
Sciences—Permanence of Paper for Printed Library Materials,
ANSI Z39.48-1992

# Dedications

This book is dedicated to my wife, Helena, and to my daughter, Sophia, duas boas razões para escrever.

# Table of Contents

# Preface

In writing this book I encountered two principal challenges. The first was that of blending my research in the areas of Paradigm Shift Theory, Modernism / Modernity and its movement toward Postmodernism / Postmodernity, and the various poetic works from which I needed to choose appropriate and illustrative samples. The second was that of including a sufficient number of examples so as to expand on notions and results presented in my previous book and articles, without placing an undo burden on the reader by way of such a plethora of writers and works so as to run the risk of missing the forest for the trees. After all, this book means to *suggest* an alternative interpretation of Iberian Poetics in their very unique context, not to disprove any of the others or even to define too specifically the process' parameters. In essence, I have relied on finding a balance between the different areas studied, a balance that I hope you, dear reader, will feel as you flip through this book's pages.

Having confronted these challenges, I have also found an unexpected joy in seeing this work come to fruition. Although relatively short, the study you are about to read represents the culmination of my thoughts to date on how Paradigm Shift Theory can be useful not only in describing the evolution of literary movements, but also in quantifying (inasmuch as would be quantifiable) the social and cultural movements from which those literary works are born.

This study's ultimate aim has and will always be to foster a greater discussion in two areas. The first, that of the epistemology of our current, rather deconstructionist and decentralizing critical methodologies, which (with few notable exceptions) has seemed to avoid the application of such an overtly categorizing theory. On the surface this worry is understandable, as literature rarely switches direction as suddenly as many scientific perspectives have over the past five centuries. Given that theory cannot apply itself in its "pure" form, but rather, as a mutable and polyvalent structure, I will posit in this study that the Iberian context lends itself to the theory insofar as this mutability holds (a notion which I will explain near the end of the work).

The second area of discussion is that of the sometimes inconspicuous links between literature (and particularly, poetic voices both in poetry and some prose) and the context which gives rise to it. Many of us who instruct and research in both literary and cultural studies know this idea as almost an axiom – no work of art has ever come (or perhaps escaped) from a vacuum. I would challenge you, dear reader, with the following notion. As our world view moves ever further from the essentialist toward something not so essentialist, and then to something else which we have tended to call the "postmodern," and later the "post-postmodern," "post-structuralist," "post-feminist," etc., we will need to endeavor to understand that that "something" reflects a much more profound process of change toward a new vision of the world, rather than as simply a novel (but not necessarily shifted) perspective within the old boundaries of what we would consider the real. Upon reading this alternative analysis, I invite you to respond as you see fit, and look forward to our future dialog.

I would also like to thank Dr. Erik Ladner for his comments, suggestions and aid in editing the original version of the text; The University Press of America for their faith in my work; Dr. William Griffin, Chair, Department of Foreign Languages, Kennesaw State University, for his unwavering support of my research; the Kennesaw State University Library for its help in tracking down lesser-known sources; Dr. Sílvia Oliveira, for her insightful comments on the translations; Dr. António Ladeira for his encouraging words; Dr. Jorge Machín Lucas for his insightful work and the writing of the foreword; and all those poets, scholars, and critics without whom a study such as this one could never have been conceived nor realized.

# Foreword

One can appreciate some constant ideas in the shift of mentality, as well as of intellectual and socio literary paradigm, during the fall of the dictatorships and the rise of democracy in Spain and Portugal during the mid 1970's. They coincide with the general traits that divide the modernism and the postmodernism. Among them, it is worth emphasizing the importance of the loss of faith in reason, in empiricism, and in technology and the heyday of unreasonableness and irrationalism, something that had been permeating worldwide after the debacle of the Second World War in 1945. The lust for evolution, for scientific novelty and for hope for a better future turns nostalgically its eyes towards the past. The search for globalizing truths is deconstructed through the ascertainment that actually the tendency toward fragmentation and the atomization of knowledge, the failure of the word to change mankind, and an absence of coherence in the systems of knowledge rule the world, the human thought and its logic.

After that epistemological watershed, the center moved towards the margins. The transcendent *logos* was replaced by an immanent and dispersed conscience and by the particular ontologies, devoid of chronological and spatial limits. Its identity was decomposed and characterized by its displacement and difficulty in fitting into our world and into our cosmos. The forms and contents were no longer an expression of a unique thought and of a hegemonic and phallocentric society and economy. There was a rehabilitation of the rights and voices of the marginalized minorities by reasons of power struggle, social class, race, gender, religion, culture or language, among other. The teleological discourses verified their apories and the indecisiveness, the uncertainty, and the ambiguities that dwelled in their interior. The referential and exoteric became self-referential and esoteric, the mimesis became semiosis, the single-voiced became multi-voiced, and the serious became playfulness, humor, irony and parody. The natural was denaturalized and tried to artificially recover the past through intertextuality, kitsch, pastiche, and simulacrum. That was a new analysis of a change of values in the gnoseologic arrogance of the northwestern, capitalist, and Christian world that must open its eyes towards its essences, its ancestors, and other identities which are not necessarily underdeveloped but different, such as the Third World, the Eastern World, Latin America, Africa, and Oceania.

The author of this excellent scholarly book, Dr. Robert Simon achieves in elaborating an insightful study of this paradigm shift or inversion in certain Iberian poets that have been producing their poetic works from the 50's to the present. Most of them have embraced both social realism and experimental techniques. There are many successes, but the most remarkable are his in depth analysis of the sociopolitical and historic coordinates and of the literary strategies of the poetic self. Very skillfully and intelligently, the scholar intellectually decolonizes preconceived ideas, many times blindly accepted by the intellectual community not because of the sense they make, but simply out of fear of punishment by the winners who hold the power.

Dr. Jorge Machín Lucas,
The University of Winnipeg,
Winnipeg, Manitoba, Canada

# Introduction: What Is The Paradigm Shift, and Why Should We Take It Seriously?

> There are two main differences between the countries of Southern Europe and those of Continental Europe. The first difference is the constant link between modernity and tradition even in political society (Sapelli, *Southern Europe since 1945,* 111).

Postmodernism is an overused term. We tend to think of it in a sort of free-for-all sense, expressing with it notions of openness to the marginalized, de-(add a verb) and / or the breaking point for Modernism / Modernity's grasp on the Western world. I, myself, have expounded rather verbosely on the subject in my previous book, *Understanding the Portuguese Poet Joaquim Pessoa, 1942-2007: A Study in Iberian Cultural Hybridity.* There I have outlined the notions of deconstruction and decentralization as the artist's principle techniques for creating a self-critical discourse. Yet, perhaps it is not the presence, but the overwhelming theorization, of such a term that has created its own deconstruction. In the works of writers such as Vasco Graça Moura and Ana Rossetti, the postmodern really fits into a larger framework, that of a multifaceted historiography reflecting some larger truth in the Iberian societies involved.

This focus on historiography, doubts about Modernism's death and / or dismemberment through postmodernism, and that "greater truth" have lead to the next point. Beyond the development of postmodernism as a response to the notion of the "master narrative" we find Kuhn's theories of the paradigm and of the paradigm shift.[1] These theories, first pertaining to the natural sciences, and adopted later in literary criticism, bring a reformulation of the idea that Postmodernism is much more than a poetic rebellion. Kuhn's principle critical work, *The Structure of Scientific Revolutions*, first questions the idea of an objective scientific view by stating that the vision of the scientist is guided by a greater set of rules through which the scientist perceives the world (8-9). This over-reaching set of rules and notions, or as Kuhn puts it, "[the] accepted model or pattern" that governs the scientific view is called a "paradigm" (Kuhn 23). The development of the modern sciences, for example, has been one of replacing one vision of the universe, or paradigm, with another, rather than an evolution of previously existing thought (23). Thus, the scientist is ruled entirely by whatever paradigm exists at the time, unable therefore to see anything which falls outside of it (24). In other words, scientific knowledge is not based upon the actual facts found; rather, it is a perception of those facts based on the dominant paradigm at the moment (Dietze 31).

As I have stated in previous scholarship on the topic, the notion that something as empirically-driven as the natural sciences could fall prey to such as subjective and decentralized phenomenon as that which paradigm theory offers does not sit easily with everyone. In fact, a debate rages among scientists as to whether they should follow this theory, also known as that of the "subjective paradigm (Bleich 320)," or that of the "objective paradigm," the traditional notion of science as a process of evolution rather than revolution (321).

The notion of the paradigm shift from the perspective of the "subjective paradigm," or the "revolution" referred to both here and in Kuhn's own work, is the process whereby one paradigm, put simply, replaces another (Dietze 34). This process works in the following three phases: 1) Crisis Phase: anomalies arise which the present paradigm cannot explain; 2) Transitional Phase: the breakdown of the paradigm becomes universally accepted; 3) The Adoption Phase, or the adoption of a new paradigm: new paradigms are created and compete until the community accepts one as the dominant paradigm (Dietze 39). Kuhn, in fact, uses several historical examples to illustrate this process, such as the discovery of oxygen (Kuhn 57). The paradigm existing at the time that oxygen was

---

1. I have discussed the theories of the Paradigm Shift in previous scholarship, namely, "The Paradigm Shift and the Evolution toward Postmodernism in Contemporary Spanish Poetry." *The South Carolina Modern Language Review*. 7.1 (2008); as well as "From the Fragmented to the Un-Centered: An Alternative Interpretation of Portuguese Poetry's Contemporary Development." *South Atlantic Review*. 74.1 (Winter 2009). 140-164.

discovered could not accept its existence, so it fell into crisis. This crisis forced science into a transitional phase, then an adoptive phase where a new paradigm that could accept the existence of oxygen was found and utilized (62).

The application of paradigm shift theory in literary criticism is a logical one, as the "subject paradigm" functions well in the context of competing, and ultimately very subjective, hermeneutical visions (Bleich 329). In fact, critical studies based on the paradigm and paradigm shift theories already exist, such as Easthope's article on Forster's *A Passage to India*, "Paradigm Lost and Paradigm Regained." (see note 1) Here Easthope detailed comparison of an empiricist's, then a post-structuralist's, critical readings of Forster's work. Easthope then analyzes the Crisis Phase, Transitional Phase and possible Adoption Phase of the most recent paradigm shift, that from High Modernism (or the literary Modernism that defined Western poetic and prosaic discourse through the first half of the Twentieth Century) into Postmodernism (or what we will call "literary postmodernism," to be defined shortly). The knowledge that pure empiricism does not function as proof of Western phallocentric superiority caused a breakdown of the paradigm prevalent up to the middle of the $20^{th}$ Century (Easthope 93). Based on Barthes' and others' criticism of the notions of the "master narrative" in both literature and literary criticism (95), a new dominant paradigm may have eventually emerged, one based on the notion that context and interpretation define a text, rather than that of a meaning embedded for the reader to find through empirical, universally accepted evidence (96-97). In sum, the purpose of the reading, and therefore, the intentions of the reader, will now define the parameters of the text's interpretation.

This focus on a paradigm shift from a relatively fixed epistemological foundation is limited to neither letters nor the sciences. According to Lynn Bloom, the field of rhetoric instruction has also suffered from a shift away from "process research" toward a multi-faceted pedagogical methodology, in which "a host of other issues and methodologies" finds an accepted space in which to exist (Bloom 35). Although the use of the term "paradigm shift" in Bloom's work (as well as in Easthope's) remains limited to the field studied, the notion that a general shift has occurred cannot be ignored. In fact, my argument during the course of this study will be to use the term in the most general sense possible—a guiding force of social, political and (of course) artistic movement from one set of principles to the next great, overreaching set. This will also differentiate this from similar studies which have used the term in a limited fashion as a replacement for "genre," "theme" or "movement" in a field-specific sense.

This study, in both scope and depth, will attempt to reconcile both theoretical and critical notions of the poetries of both the time-period and place in question (the Iberian Peninsula, approx. 1950-2000) with Kuhn's theories of the Paradigm Shift. It is my hope that, by crossing the evolution of the postmodern with that of the new paradigm as first outlined by Easthope and developed here, we may better understand the forces at work in both the greater movement between esthetic preferences in poetry and the undertakings of the particular poets involved, and the socio-political forces which these poetic processes reflect. We must be careful, however, not to fall into the same trap which seems to encompass Easthope's perspective, that of a narrowly focused, literary definition for the paradigm shift. Again, by removing ourselves from recent debates and returning to Kuhn's original definition, we are able to see poetry's place, and not its dominance, within a larger system.

In essence, then, the application of the Paradigm Shift theory allows for the inclusion of all aspects of a culture's evolution and expression in the diachronic context of that society's movement from one state to another, socially, politically, and artistically. It grants us the ability to view culture and literature as a singular series of processes moving toward a common end or goal, perhaps even a common destiny.

The second question to address is that of this introduction's title: Why should we take any of this seriously? In other words, are we simply over-theorizing and over-simplifying an extremely complex situation in late 20th Century Western cultures? I believe the answer to these questions is two-fold. First, a study such as this strives to appreciate the complexity of the time and space in which these events, both socio-politically and literarily, occur. By removing the multiple perspectives of the era we may come to precisely the same simplified conclusions that we intend to most heartily avoid. Second, and just as importantly, if there truly is a paradigm shift occurring in Iberian society, and if that shift is so well reflected and documented in Iberian poetries that even a book such as this one is possible, then poetry's utility in defining social phenomena must be recognized. In a world which has chosen other "bestseller" literary forms, including novels and film, over the poetic word, the people of our day and age may be cutting off their nose to spite their face by ignoring poetry's importance in a larger scale. And if there be (or not be) greater conclusions to find, and / or other ideas about our world that these poets and their work may have revealed to us without our explicit knowledge, I have the hope that the theories of the Paradigm Shift, as a cornerstone for understanding poetry's role in a wider world context, may take their rightful place of importance given that the peoples of the

Iberian nations have become preoccupied with just such questions both literarily and culturally (Iarocci 43).

Having said that, let us look at what the two principle paradigms we will discuss, the Modern paradigm (not to be confused with terms such as Modernism and "modernismo" in the literary sense, although these phases of literature do play an important part in the discussion of paradigm shifts) and the possible Postmodern paradigm, are composed of. This, as scientific a study as it may seem abstract, will give us a clearer view of the rules which both govern the world of before and during the 1950s, as those rules' breakdown and subsequent surrendering to the Postmodern tendencies of the 1970s to the end of the 20th Century. Again, the shift may not actually be toward what we will define as the "Postmodern paradigm" (I use quotes to be specific as much as to create a sense of irony), but rather toward something else.

The Modern paradigm is, in essence, the result of a sort of agglutination of several cultural, political, social and artistic changes in Western European societies beginning with the period we have designated as the Late Medieval Period and evolving quickly into the subsequently named Renaissance (roughly from the middle of the 15th through the early 16th Centuries). "La modernidad nace y se desarrolla en el centro de Europa y se va extendiendo en círculos concéntricos al resto de la humanidad, en procesos denominados *planetización, universalización y globalización* (Pinedo 41)." (Eng., "Modernity is born and develops in the center of Europe and reaches out in concentric circles to the rest of humanity, in processes called *planetization, universalization and globalization.*") Although visible in a variety of areas, one of the most evident would be that of the development of Western educational ideals:

> Desde la perspectiva de la Filosofía de la educación, se podría afirmar que gran parte de los fines educativos que la modernidad asume, se apuntaron desde el Renacimiento a través de una selección que con el tiempo se truncó en subrayar unos objetivos en detrimento de otros, rompiéndose el ideal de armonía acerca del hombre y de la humanidad que inspiró la génesis del pensamiento humanista.
> (Martínez de Soria 47-8)

> (Eng. "From the perspective of Educational Philosophy, one could affirm that the better part of the educational goals that Modernity espouses, came from the Renaissance by way of a selection that, with time, was truncated in underlining some objectives to the detriment of others, breaking with the ideal of harmony of man and humanity that inspired the genesis of humanist thought
> (Translation by Robert Simon).

Since then, its seemingly multifaceted forms have not varied from certain central ideals based on the notion of Humanism in the spirit of Erasmus, and on the notion of "an exaggerated esteem for novelty with disdain for tradition (Orringer 135)." By Orringer's definition, then, even the Baroque may be considered part of Modernity, and thus, part of the Modern paradigm (this goes against Kaup's assertion that "modernity is haunted by the return of its antithetical, premodern other: the baroque (Kaup 221)"). Humanism can be defined, then, in terms of the harmonious inner workings of the human being (to which Martínez de Soria has alluded) and as the individual's realization that the world around him is not a concrete and immutable object, but a series of interpretations made so that the world may then suit the needs of the individual. The notion of an essential truth as placed within the interpretive nature of the human experience, then, forms the basis for the Modern paradigm's various permutations over time. Even the Romantic social revolutions of the 19th Century and the Modernist (using the non-Hispanic definition of the term) artistic manifestations of the fin-de-siècle and first decades of the 20th Century such as Fauvism, Dadaism and Surrealism do not escape these, among other, fundamentally accepted social, political and artistic assertions. In essence, "its beginning is difficult to locate, but it has been variously assigned to the late medieval period, the Renaissance, or the Enlightenment. Its dynamic qualities make it hard to pin down: modernity unfolds as a process developing and changing over time (Grady 2)." Of course, my assertion goes against what Longhurst, as well as Juan Ramón Jiménez, has called Hispanic and non-Hispanic Modernisms *as a point of contrast* to the previous movements within Modernity, "a broad movement that affected the whole of Western culture and which was based on changing patterns of thought (Longhurst 265)." It is until the Second World War that the Modern paradigm, thus, remains only slightly modified and essentially unchallenged.

The Postmodern paradigm, if it may be called that, may be studied and understood through two distinctive facets: social Postmodernity and literary postmodernism. We may characterize social Postmodernity as the absence of an essential socio-political identity. Ironically, if, as Álvares puts it, "modern discourse is characterised by a permanent . . . separation, which cannot be mended [, then] from this perspective, the postmodern emphasis on fragmentation and disunity derives from within modernity itself (95)." The loss of the absolute connection between the signifier and the signified (94), along with notions of deconstruction and decentralization which we wills study in the following paragraphs, also give Postmodernity (and literary postmodernism) both a commonality with, and its essential point of separation, from Modernity. As a result,

we see a resurgence of the notion that we become affiliated with a con-
cept of belonging, rather than the Modern paradigm's notion of owing
allegiance by "filiations," or birth, into that group.

In terms of literary postmodernism, a wide range of critical work has
aided us in defining what has attempted to remain indefinable. Nonethe-
less, a widely accepted definition for the postmodern poetic is given in
Linda Hutcheon's well-known synthesis of postmodern criticism, *A Po-
etics of Postmodernism.*[2] Here, she defines it as "a contradictory phe-
nomenon, one that uses and abuses, installs and then subverts, the very
concept it challenges . . . " (3). It serves at its advent to demystify the
notion of the "master narrative" as proposed by Lyotard (whether that be
an historical, literary or cultural one), through the process whereby "con-
sensus becomes the illusion of consensus" (Hutcheon 6-7). Postmodern-
ism, at its most basic level, desires to counter modernist discourse (which
we study here as the final stage of the Modern paradigm's literary ex-
pression) by removing the authority vested in the text and replace it with
the revelation of that text's true status, as a human construct, both ex-
pressed and limited by the language used to create it (7-8). Thus, any
discourse, whether artistic or political, may be understood as nothing
more than the manifestation of a "contradictory interaction" based on any
given ideology and its "relations of power" with the reader / listener
(178-179). Techniques such as intertextuality may serve to reveal the
true nature of the "master narrative" as a combination of the literary and
the historical. "It is a kind of seriously ironic parody that often enables
this contradictory doubleness: the intertexts of history and fiction take on
parallel status in the parodic reworking of the textual past of both the
'world' and literature" (124). This world of intertextuality supports the
reworking of particular "master narratives," such as phallocentric and
political hegemonies, decentralizing them and, thus, leaving their rela-
tive, and even illusory, nature exposed (158-159).

The single most important artistic technique employed in the poetry
of postmodernism is alluded to multiple times in the previous paragraph,
that is, deconstruction. In his work *On Deconstruction*, Culler names
three principal aspects of deconstruction (Culler 85-89). First, the decon-
structive text must work *within* the terms of the same system it means to
deconstruct. In this way, the text will *undermine* the notion, idea, philos-
ophy or base text which it at first would seem to assert. Second, and
more specifically, the deconstructive text will *question* the notion of cau-

---

2. In fact, what follows is based on a summary of literary postmodernism which appears
in my previous book, *Understanding the Portuguese Poet Joaquim Pessoa: a Study in
Iberian Cultural Hybridity* (the Edwin Mellen Press, 2008).

sality in the deconstructed object. This means that the text will make evident the relationship between *cause* and *effect* in which the main ideas of the deconstructed object create its logical base. Finally, the deconstructive text will *reverse* the hierarchical oppositions of the original causal scheme. Thus, by inverting the system in which the deconstructed object works, it may subvert the effectiveness of the causality which feeds the notion of hierarchy sustaining the object. As Hutcheon states, "postmodernism might be seen to operate as an internalized challenge to analytic-referential discourse by pointing to the way in which its model of infinite expression is, in fact . . . , underpinned by a drive toward totalization and finite and closed knowledge" (75).

The application of this technique in any text causes the illusion of the text as a "master narrative" to be undone. Returning to the defining characteristic of deconstruction, through the process outlined above, the "modern" text, or "master narrative," becomes just another example of a value-laden hierarchy with no real central core to sustain it. Thus, the text is not only deconstructed, it becomes decentralized.

Decentralization, in fact, appears in some of the first, and most influential, critical texts in the study of postmodernism. Roland Barthes, in his work *Mythologies*, describes language as nothing more than a small part of a greater, yet identical, structure of signifier, signified and sign. "In myth, we find again the tri-dimensional pattern which I have just described [in a summary of Saussurean linguistic theory]: the signifier, the signified and the sign. But myth is a peculiar system, in that it is constructed from a semiological chain which existed before it: it *is a second-order system*" (Barthes 114). Ultimately, the semiotic of myth is identical to that of language, meaning that both are finite constructions based on the same, limited model within and through which the illusion of form exist merely as a function of its own limitations. For this reason, what Barthes calls form (117) is not the object itself, but that into which the "impoverished," empty shell that our linguistic / mythological / sociological tri-partite conception converts it. As Culler puts it, Barthes works toward the ideal of considering all human endeavor as just another linguistic system, "as a series of 'languages'" that serve to uncover cultural secrets (Culler, *At the Boundaries*, 30-31).

Jacques Derrida explains the technique (or "project") of deconstruction as a way of both undoing textual phallocentrism (Harvey 196) and of revealing "différance," or "a system of difference and contradiction" (Derrida 44) which deconstruction exploits. As postmodernism suggests that no text may contain, nor exist as, a "master narrative," the only centralizing force in such a text becomes that of Derrida's "différance." This re-definition of the notion of a universal center as nothing more than a contrast between differing textual elements, implies that no real definitions may exist, which leads then to a questioning of the nature of literature versus non-literature (i.e., history, political discourse, etc.) Derrida's *Glas*, a simultaneous literary and philosophical discourse, effectively demonstrates this notion (Culler, *At the Boundaries*, 38).

In terms of Derrida's push for a deconstruction of phallocentric language, other critics have taken up the struggle to deconstruct and decentralize this notion. Julia Kristeva, for example, takes up the argument in terms of the marginalization of women in the now-derided notion of the "master narrative." In her *Revolution in Poetic Language*, Kristeva studies the grammar of poetic language and resolves that it functions to express "significance" not through normative discourse, which capitalist society has stratified and appropriated, but through a marginalized discourse. "Magic, shamanism, esoterism, the carnival, and 'incomprehensible' poetry all underscore the limits of socially useful discourse and attest to what it represses: the *process* that exceeds the subject and his communicative structures" (Kristeva 30). The term "significance," thus, represents the true nature of the world, a "structuring and de-structuring *practice*" rather than a set hierarchy (31). Rhythm (36) and the phonic quality of language (37), both of which reflect poetry's underlying primitive structure, also represent both the womb and its "significance," movement and origin. The term Kristeva designates to this phenomenon is that of the "chora," a Greek term for "womb" (35-36). It defines both the derridean "différance," or the relationship between the real "and the symbolic," and the element which links the body to its origin, "the mother" that gave birth to it (36-37). This area of postmodernism will become evident in our studies of the poets from 1980 onward.

The anti-phallic struggle is not the only one present in postmodernism, however. The fight against capitalist government (and against the hierarchical nature of capitalism in general) and the false freedom it offers becomes a primary concern for some postmodern critics. For example, Terry Eagleton, in his work *An Introduction to Literary Theory*, explains that, just as the notion of a literary canon is a social construction (22-23) and an exercise of power in a hegemonic relationship between the reader and the critic (240), so would be political discourse, particularly a discourse borne of capitalist regimes whose "master narrative" is nothing more than an expression of their own tyranny (246). In Eagleton's view, the notions of literature and of literary criticism are really just social constructions (242), an opinion which, with the support of deconstruction's result of decentralization, makes sense, since no universal center, whether historical or literary, really exists.

As we have previous stated, this study will focus its energy on the application of specific poets' themes and work toward an overall application of Kuhn's theory of the Paradigm Shift. The chapters are divided by era: first, the 1950s though the impressive social changes occurring in Peninsular society up to the fall of the dictatorships in 1974 and 1975; afterwards, the seeming acceptance of postmodernism / postmodernity during the first years of the democratic period and following until the end of the 1980s; and finally, what will appear to be a return to a mutated essentialist discourse in the 1990s (as well as the continuation of this discourse into the first decade of the new Century). Each chapter will begin with a summary of the social and political forces at work in each era, turning then to the poets for examples. From the 1950s and 1960s we study António Ramos Rosa and Herberto Helder in Portugal, José Hierro and Ángel González in Spain. From the 1970s and continuing to the 1980s we will focus our attention on the poetry of Ruy Belo and Vasco Graça Moura in Portugal, then on Ana Rossetti and the poetic prose of Belén Gopegui in Spain. (See note 2) Finally, our focus will shift toward the mystical, yet strongly postmodern, poetics of Clara Janés (in Spain) and Joaquim Pessoa (in Portugal), proving a growing link between the two country's poetic trajectories in both the seemingly dominant Post-modern paradigm and the counter-current to them, forcing us to re-examine our notion of exactly what kind of paradigm is really dominant in the Iberian cultures. I have chosen to forgo the temptation to give multiple examples for each period, as this study means not to be the definitive argument toward Paradigm Shift theory's application in Iberia; rather, it suggests that an alternative reading of the past several decades' poetic and social evolution is more than possible.

It should also be noted that, to those who have read my previous work on this and other topics, the examples shown will look rather familiar. This is because, and I admit it openly, much of the work in this study is a re-formulation of previous work on various topics in Spanish and Portuguese literatures and cultures which I have published in various forms over the past several years. I will state plainly, then, that although much of the analysis seen in this study is not original to the study itself, the recontextualization of these examples into this alternative vision of social, political and literary evolution in Spain and Portugal will make the old seem new (or seem old again, depending upon just how postmodern your own view is these days). As the wise used to say, "if you don't have to reinvent the wheel, then don't." In following that advice I present to you, the esteemed reader, this study whose very structure, in its constant denaturalization and re-centralization of theory and text, is as Iberian postmodern as the Peninsula itself.

In sum, it is the poetry written to express the space between the failing of the former paradigm and the surging forth of the latter that will be our principle area of interest. In seeing how the paradigm shift has occurred (or, as we will soon see, may still be occurring), and how it becomes manifest in the poetry of the Iberian countries, we gain greater insight into how concrete historical fact may point directly toward the larger, abstract concepts that guide us.

# Chapter I: 1955 to 1974, António Ramos Rosa and Herberto Helder

By the 1950s Modernism in Portuguese society, politics and art is in danger. Its principle representative works have become tokens of the regime which utilizes their nationalistic tone as a banner for Salazar's xenophobic governmental and horribly stratified social structures. In fact, although change has already begun to occur, for the most part this societal stratification is the norm—a small oligarchy rules over a largely rural and consistently abused working class. Literary works of the first Neo-Realists, such as Alves Redol's *Gaibéus* (1939), have done little in the mostly suppressed struggle to alleviate the situation.

Portugal in this period was a nation still under the dominance of the Salazar dictatorship which had taken power in the 1920s (we should note that he was not elected President officially until 1932). Although admitted into the United Nations in 1955, the country was considered a "non-democratic" state (Birmingham 167). Over the following two decades, leading to the emergence of democracy in Portugal in 1974, the government found itself forced to open outside artistic and political influences while simultaneously attempting to hold onto a colonial empire in a world war for which its military was poorly equipped (168).

It is this colonial war which leaves the deepest marks on Portuguese society over the course of the period. "In 1963 the Colonial War brought more dramatic changes to Portugal's social culture than the world war had brought in 1943. The ultra-conservative social traditions of the 'grande bourgeoisie' were gradually eased after surviving both world wars in Edwardian isolation and splendour (169)." This was due to a loss of manual labor due to the drafting of troops to fight in the war, along with the emigration of a large portion of the urban and rural labor forces to more developed urban centers in Western Europe such as Paris (169-171). The industrialization of the country also cannot be ignored – the welcoming of foreign businesses and the rise of "a new generation of Portuguese entrepreneurs" aided in the growth of this sector of the economy (172-3). Thus, a new economic reality of a small but growing white-collar sector and greater capacity of movement within the population began to emerge (similarly to that of Spain, which we will study in the next Chapter). It must also be noted that, while some prosperity reached certain areas of the populace, the majority remained in abject poverty, subject to the whims of larger land-owners (Birmingham 171). This created a space for disenchantment and growing dissent within the population.

The evolution of literature in this period reflects well the notions of rebirth, economic growth and inequality, and disenchantment with both the social context of 1950s-70s Portugal as well as the form by which literature has defined this context. By 1950, the Surrealist movement in Portugal had ended and two groups of poets took predominance in Portugal.

The first, the so-called "neo-realists," had actually formed in the 1930s (and whose survivors continue writing currently). They tended to focus on social issues as the prime theme of literature. This group of writers included Irene Lisboa, José Rodrigues Miguéis in the 1930s, Alves Redol in the 1930s and 40s (mentioned above), and Joaquim Namorado in the 1950s. The literary magazine *Vertice*, founded in the 1940s, symbolized the social focus of this group.

The other group, known as the experimentalists, was linked more closely with the defunct Surrealist movement to try to recreate an essential notion of art as a reflection of influences and processes both external and internal to the self. This group of poets included names such as Herberto Helder, Luíza Neto Jorge, Ana Hatherly and Fiama Hasse Pais Brandão. *Poesia 61* serves as the obra magna of this group, representative of the experimental, or Concrete, poets in their search, "a procura de uma linguagem que, num ou noutro caso, se torna fundamentalmente substantiva (Guimarães, *A Poesia Contemporânea*, 87)" (Eng., "the search for a language that, in one or another case, becomes fundamentally substantive"). Poets such as Jorge de Sena and António Ramos Rosa may be linked to the experimentalists, although their poetries contain a heavy influence from the Modernist poets of the "Renascença" and of "Orpheu" at turn of the Twentieth century (as we will soon see in the case of the latter). Although both groups of poets worked heavily with social issues, it is clear that while the former group emphasized social issues as the raison d'être of contemporary poetry, the latter emphasized the use of new and experimental forms, techniques and thematic approaches to writing as a more suitable vehicle for "containing poetic language" which the previous generations of poets had "dispersed" (87), and thus, expressing the changing dynamics which defined their Portugal. This strong desire for change, in competition with the more direct style of the Neo-Realists, is one of the classic markers of the Paradigm Shift's first phase, known as the Crisis Phase.

In order that we may understand better how this Crisis Phase is reflected in the actual writing of the time, I have chosen two writers on whom to focus. The first, António Ramos Rosa, is linked intimately with the experimentalists as well as with more mystical and "fin-de-siècle" tendencies in Portugal. The latter, Herberto Helder, reveals himself to be an integral part of the experimentalist movement.

In the work of poets such as António Ramos Rosa [and other contributors to the magazine *Árvore* (Guimarães, *A Poesia Contemporânea*, 10)], we may observe a certain recycling of the Surrealist poetic style of the 1940s. This happens so that one may create (or in this case, re-create) a new poetic in which the universal could find its expression (29). Rosa's work tries to combine the Neo-Realism of the 1930s and 40s with Surrealism, making poetry an "acto total," a uniquely complete humanized poetry (17). Despite this daring combination, he is described as a rather "restrained" poet, attempting to concentrate language in such as way that all words may contain a universal meaning, such as in his *O Grito Claro* (1958) and *Incêndio dos Aspectos* (1980), the latter of which is described as more metapoetic than Surrealist (Gusmão 166).

As can be seen in Rosa's "Poema dum Funcionário Cansado," from *O Grito Claro*, the combination of the common-man's plight with that of the immediacy found in surrealist symbolism leads toward an attempt to understand better the nature of the universe as a whole:

A noite trocou-me os sonhos e as mãos
dispersou-me os amigos
tenho o coração confundido e a rua é estreita

Estreita em cada passo
as casas engolem-nos
sumimo-nos
estou num quarto só num quarto só
com os sonhos trocados
com toda a vida às avessas a arder num quarto só

Sou um funcionário apagado
um funcionário triste
a minha alma não acompanha a minha mão
Débito e Crédito Débito e Crédito

a minha alma não dança com os números
tento escondê-la envergonhado
o chefe apanhou-me com o olho lírico na gaiola do quintal em frente
e debitou-me na minha conta de empregado
Sou um funcionário cansado dum dia exemplar
Porque não me sinto orgulhoso de ter cumprido o meu dever?
Porque me sinto irremediavelmente perdido no meu cansaço?

Soletro velhas palavras generosas
Flor rapariga amigo menino
irmão beijo namorada
mãe estrela música

São as palavras cruzadas do meu sonho
palavras soterradas na prisão da minha vida
isto todas as noites do mundo uma noite só comprida
num quarto só
       (Mendes (ed.), *O Poeta na Rua*, 22-23)

(Eng.
The night switched my dreams and my hands
It sent my friends in every which direction
My heart is confused and the road is narrow

Narrow at each step
The houses swallow us
We vanish
I am alone in a room alone in a room
with the dreams switched
with my whole life turned around burning alone in a room

I am a wilted clerk
a sad clerk
my soul does not accompany my hand
Debit and Credit Debit and Credit
my soul does not dance with the numbers
I try to hid it ashamed
the boss caught me with a lyrical eye on the cage of the front yard
and charged it to my employee payroll
I am a clerk tired of exemplary days
Why don't I feel proud to have accomplished my duty?
Why do I feel irremediably lost in my exhaustion?

I spell out old generous words
Flower girl friend boy
brother kiss girlfriend
mother star music

They are crosswords in my dream
words buried in the prison of my life

this all the world's nights just one long night
alone in a room.)
(Translation by Robert Simon)

The first stanza of the poem introduces the poetic subject, an emotionally exhausted office-worker who has begun to feel trapped and isolated. This is not only a spatial isolation, as emphasized in the "rua estreita" ("narrow road") of the first stanza and in the repetition of the phrase "num quarto só" ("alone in a room") in the second stanza, but an emotional one as well. He feels confused and somewhat hopeless, as seen in the third stanza where he questions his own emotional reaction toward a job for which he thinks he should feel "orgulhoso" ("proud"). In the fourth stanza the poetic subject, having hit an existential barrier, begins writing a series of words whose seemingly random order is reminiscent of the surrealist "automated writing" style in which semantic connections could be made through superficially unrelated words. Here, the words "flower girl friend boy / brother kiss girlfriend / mother star music" link the mundane, mortal and human (the "girl," "boy," "brother," "girlfriend") with the ephemeral, such as the notion of love, the supra-physical aspect of music and the greatness of the cosmos. Their combined meanings represent the "intercrossed words of my dreams" which, as stated in the fifth stanza, contrast the utter hopelessness he feels in "the prison" of his life, reflected in the return to the "quarto" in which he physically resides.

As Rosa's poetic work developed over the next three decades, the presence of certain Romantic-period myths began to emerge. This creates a scenario in which the theme of "Animism" (present in Saudosista works such as those of Teixeira de Pascoaes) combines comfortably with what we see is an already strong Surrealist symbolism. "O possível animismo que se pode entrever em alguns passos da poesia de Ramos Rosa nunca é de natureza alegorizante, como tantas vezes acontece com os poetas ligados ao Saudosismo; aponta, antes, para uma concretização simbólica que lhe dá uma ambiguidade, um pulsar de sentidos diversificados" (Guimarães, *A Poesia da Presença*, 25). (Eng. "The possible Animism that can be perceived in some points in the poetry of Rosa is never of an allegorical nature, as is so often seen in the poets connected with Saudosismo; it indicates, rather, a symbolic concretization that gives it an ambiguity, a pulsing of diversified sentiment).[3] This multiplic-

---

3. "Saudosismo" was a poetic movement at the turn of the Twentieth Century, characterized by a Symbolist-like sublimation of the poetic word and by the overpowering sentiment of nostalgia known as "saudade." It served as both a mode of expression for the

ity of meanings makes sense, as in many cases Rosa uses the past to express that past's future, or the present, thus integrating the past and the present in an ever-renewing cycle of life and of the poetic word. "O poema que encerrava [*O Grito Claro*] deixava inscrito no pretérito aquilo que, de facto, se revelaria futuro, ao transformar-se numa espécie de programa poético ao longo dos anos: a procura de um lugar de palavras (e para as palavras) por forma a integrá-las num horizonte sempre interrogado e renovado de vida" (Mendes 11). (Eng. "The poem completing [the *O Grito Claro*] registered in the past ["preterit"][4] what, in fact, would be revealed as future, upon transforming itself into a kind of poetic doctrine as the years went by: the search for a place of words (and for words) as a manner of integrating them into a scrutinized horizon and renewed with life.") The work of Herberto Helder, a contemporary of Rosa's, serves as an example of Marinho's claim of multiplicity while simultaneously embodying the notion that the poetic word simply does not serve to express meaning and universality in the way in which Rosa attempts (Marinho 41).

Herberto Helder began writing in the 1950s, as did Rosa. However, while Rosa maintained a vision better associated with universality, at least until the 1970s (Marinho 47), Helder became well-known as an "experimental" poet, visualizing poetry as a "máquina de emaranhar palavras e frases" ("machine to tangle words and phrases") rather than as an expression of the universal essence (Martinho 18). Although it is possible to divide his work into three distinct phases, those of a lyrical, then prosaic and finally metaphorical poetry, his main themes throughout are love and the metapoetic discussion of artistic creation (Perkins 4). Helder's poetry remains in the present tense, as for the poet the present is all that really exists (Ferreira 170), creating a timeless, mythical space which is both rooted in a Surrealist natural symbolism and fixation on a single moment, such as is observed in this excerpt from his famous erotic work "O Amor em Visita," (Perkins 3-4):

> Dai-me uma jovem mulher com sua harpa de sombra
> e seu arbusto de sangue. Com ela
> encantarei a noite.

---

feelings of betrayal against the Portuguese monarchy, who, in 1890, ceded the central regions of the southern African colonies to the British in what as known as the "ultimatum," as well as a starting point for the Neo-Romantic tendencies of many modernist poets.

4. Literally, a completed and finished past.

Dai-me uma folha viva de erva, uma mulher.
Seus ombros beijarei, a pedra pequena
do sorriso de um momento.
Mulher quase incriada, mas com a gravidade
de dois seios, com o peso lúbrico e triste
de boca. Seus ombros beijarei.
(Helder, *Poesia Toda*, 31)

(Eng.
Give me a young woman with her shadow harp
And her blood-bush. With her
I will enchant the night.
Give me a leaf alive with herb, a woman.
I will kiss her shoulders, the small stone
of a moment's smile.
An almost feral woman, but with the gravity
of two breasts, with her sad and lubric weight
of mouth. Her shoulders I will kiss.)

In this first stanza of the poem it is evident that the poetic subject's erotic desires toward the woman become encapsulated in a mythical yet simultaneously surrealist symbolism. Despite not having reached the negation of time seen in works such as *Os Passos em Volta* (Ferreira 170), the presence of the surrealist style is clear. In fact, Helder's ultimate goals are the Surrealist liberation, or "libertação," of the poetic word and the simultaneous finding of it. "Na sua escrita privilegiam-se as duas vertentes – a criadora e a mágica – da poesia, como se ela fosse efectivamente animada ou, mesmo, habitada pelas duas grandes poéticas . . .: a da *libertação* e a do *encontro das palavras*" (Guimarães, *A Poesia Contemporânea*, 68) (Eng. "In his writing two trends are privileged – the magical and creative one – that of poetry, as though it were, in effect, alive or, even, inhabited by the two great poetics . . .: that of *freeing* and that of the *encounter of words*.") As in the stanza cited above, the erotic encounter is linguistic – it happens in a future that, although it has not come to pass, is referred to in detail. The presence of the "chora" is also observable in this stanza, as the connection between the woman and nature in the fourth verse alludes to her place both as a part of the greater scheme of life and as an essential element of it. His attempt at a physical union, then, may carry him to the origin of his own life. It is this origin, or the maternal presence in his poetry, that forms the center of his own original mythology (Cruz 136).

However, the uncontrolled syntactic and semantic movement found abundantly in his work suggests a loss of any fixed significance to poetic language, allowing the notion of meaning, as Guimarães puts it, to be inverted. Thus, the universal, through a freeing of language, becomes the signifier for a ludic meaning.[5] This is seen in texts such as "Texto 10" from *Antropofagias*:

Encontro-me na posição de estar freneticamente suspenso
das "cenas" nos fundos da "noite"
algum "teatro" vem declarar-se pronto para as suas "leituras"
o "movimento" procura o "corpo"
propriamente
permissivo limpo uma "biografia" de animal
feita
da sua fome e sede e da sua viagem "até onde"
"lugares" encontrados "narrativas" a ocupar uma "atenção última"
a flor que se organizou de um povoamento
de "esforços" florais "tentativas" erros riquíssimos
a cena traz ondas de treva o silêncio que a "tradição" manda: . . .
    (*Poesia Toda*, 526)

(Eng. I find myself in the position of being frenetically suspended
from the "scenes" in the depths of the "night"
some "theatre" come to declare itself ready for its "readings"
"movement" searches for "body"
properly
permissive clean an animal "biography"
made
from its hunger and thirst and from its voyage "toward where"
found "places" "narratives" occupying a "ultimate attention"
the flower that was organized by a settlement
from floral "efforts" "attempts" rich errors
the scene brings dark waves the silence that "tradition" demands: . . .)

In this text, one in which the singular use of the present tense denotes timelessness, terms such as "cenas" and "noite" are placed in quotation marks to designate a supposed meaning of each term within this timeless, boundless space. As the text moves forward, however, the differentiation between theatrical, textual and non-artistic spaces becomes confused and

---

5. "À sintaxe convencional é anteposto um espaço de visão—criado pela disposição gráfica das palavras ou letras—ou todo um processo combinatório, pelo qual se encadeiam, cruzam, substituem ou se invertem as palavras; é a «beleza assintáctica». O *significado*—que se perdeu ou, pelo menos, tende a perder-se—é substituído pelo *sentido* lúdico" (Guimarães 69) (Eng. "A space of vision counters conventional syntax—created by the graphic displacement of words or letters—or an entire combinatory system, through which words are chained, crossed, substituted or inverted; it is «asyntactic beauty [beauty resulting from a deviation from syntax]». *Meaning*—that was lost or, at least, tends to become lost – is substituted by ludic *sense*.")

indefinable. Here we see, then, the first real signs of a postmodern poetic in Portugal, as the Surrealist notion of freedom becomes a tool for a process of semantic carnivalization of language reminiscent of deconstruction. Its loss of an original meaning, despite the presence of the search for the "chora," in Helder's manipulation of Surrealism's imagery also decentralizes the poetic word.

Let us return to the notion of the Paradigm Shift. As we have seen, this period in Portuguese history and literary evolution has seen a change from the consolidated dictatorship to one which has had to cede control in the areas of commerce to a small middle class. The upper class of Portuguese society, in which the oligarchic, ruling class consists, has seen its power base diminish due to a lacking labor supply conscripted to military service.

It is a moment of Crisis for the Modern paradigm in Portugal— Modernism, whose legacy from Pessoa's *Mensagem* had served to bolster the nationalistic feelings that the ruling class espoused, has found itself criticized by the bourgeoning group of literary mavericks known as the "experimentalists," as well as by the Neo-Realists (a representative of whom, Joaquim Pessoa, we will study in relative detail in a subsequent chapter). The political message that the government has disseminated does not convince these artists – through new forms and topics, social issues such as dictatorship and poverty are treated in a context of direct conflict with the ruling class.

To this we must add the presence of texts which speak to the abuses of the Colonial Wars. Thousands of native Angolans and Mozambicans were murdered during the 1960s, at first by Portuguese soldier, and later by "black conscripts paid to defend the colony against their own kith and kin (Birmingham 176)." Despite the economic boost the Colonial Wars gave Portugal in this era, as well as several victories won against the rebels in Angola and Mozambique, by 1974 many junior officers of the Portuguese army, upon reading Spínola's latest publication, decided they had had enough of the war (178).

As we can see, there is ample proof in these developments during the 1950s and 60s to indicate that the Modern paradigm, which in its nationalist fervor has allowed for the dictatorship and colonial situation to occur, finds itself under increasing pressure. The poetic representations of this Modernism, those of the *Renascença, Orpheu* and *Presença* groups, ironically aided in leading Portugal to a government whose abuses of the populations under its domain no longer found justification in nationalism and isolationism. The countercurrent to the political message of the government comes, thus, from poets such as Ramos Rosa and Helder. The former serves this purpose for his combining of the mystical with a Neo-Realist preoccupation with social stratification and an intimation of the self; the latter, for his entirely internal struggle with the self in an environment where the self becomes lost in the tattered remnants of the essential.

In this context, it fits to say that the Modern paradigm within the Portuguese context is caught plainly in the Crisis Phase, according to Kuhn's Theory. To review, Kuhn postulated that the Crisis Phase occurs when a paradigm no longer is able to explain, express or justify a new reality. In the Portugal of this period this is very definitely the case. The political situation and the philosophy of the dictatorship find themselves in conflict as much with each other as with the external forces that have begun to shape Portuguese society in accordance with Western European norms. Beyond that, at least two major literary forms have sprung up to challenge the nationalism that has defined Portuguese literary Modernism during the previous decades—the Neo-Realists (now as a major force in literature, not just in a secondary fashion) and the Experimentalists, examples of whom we have seen here. Of course, there exists in this period a group of pro-Salazar traditionalists known by the designation of their principle magazine, *Távola Redonda*. Their function was to defend the existing political and social system of suppression and stratification. However, it is in this period that the group's voice is subsumed under that of the two formerly mentioned groups. In this way we see that there is not only a Paradigm Shift in an abstract sense in Portugal, but that we can observe clear and definitive proof of this shift at the social, political and literary levels.

Yet, we must be careful not to say that the Crisis Phase begins in the 1950s without seeing that there exist antecedents to it. The recognition of Modernism's passing through the approximation of the poetic subject and the poet, in contrast to the former's distinctive separation, as is the case of Fernando Pessoa and his heteronyms (Mendes 8), serves also to indicate that poetry in Portugal is in its Crisis Phase. It is possible to add that, according to Marinho, the plurality of voices heard in Portuguese poetry in the 1960s reflects the failure of the poetic word as an efficient and useful tool for expressing meaning and universality (Marinho 41).

In focusing on the two writers studied in this chapter, it becomes clear that the Crisis Phase also evolves quickly into the first stages of a Transition Phase (whose details we will discuss in the next two chapters). We may see Rosa's poetry, at least in the 1950s and 60s, to be one of the final, all-encompassing breaths of Modernism in Portugal, one which attempts to conciliate the differing ideologies present and salvage their essential universality. It should also be clear that Helder's work represents the voice of both universality (hence, the mythical path his poetry takes) and skepticism concerning the possibility of absolute expression through language. His poetry indicates a fluidity of meaning made manifest through language's inability to support the universal meaning that a poet like Rosa thought that it should. Helder's treatment of his romantic relationships with women in his poetry is one based on an impersonal symbolism, rather than on the notion of commitment found in many of his contemporaries (Perkins 4). Given the invention of a singular, mythical universality in his poetry, rather than the presence of a pre-conceived notion of an essential, universal foundation, this makes sense. In any case, the development of both Rosa's and Helder's poetries in the 1950s and 60s indicates that, although Portuguese poetry at this time finds itself in the Crisis Phase, characteristics of the Transition Phase appearing through Helder's use of techniques which match clearly with the Postmodern paradigm that takes a dominant position in the 1970s.

To recap, as the dictatorial regime in Portugal in the 1950s begins to weaken, the social fabric which as supported it also finds itself under pressure to change. The general populace, particularly the working classes but also the middle and upper class, is more disenchanted over time with the empty promises of unity and peace in the Portuguese Empire, considering the toll the Colonial Wars takes on both the working classes numbers and productivity. At the same time, foreign influences begin to filter into the country (in a fashion similar to that of the "fin-de-siècle" period, although with greater acceptance than at the time of the *Renascença* movement due to the reasons listed above) with consequences in both the social and literary realms. This change may be seen in the poetry of the time, whose forms and themes take non-traditional and very critical stances against the regime and its oligarchic social structure. Although not sufficient to incite rebellion, these new literary forms do have the effect of creating a space for challenging the existing regime both politically and socially.

As Modernism loses its ability to explain the new reality confronting the Portuguese State, its population and its artists, the need for a new over-arching set of concepts to define this new reality is more recognizable. The same holds for the literature that reflects and represents abstractly these entities. The small literary rebellions that the new Neo-Realist and Experimentalist writers represent do not truly threaten the status quo of the Portuguese regime, at least until the early 1970s when even the military can no longer justify the Caetano government's stance on the rather unsuccessful Colonial War situation (Birmingham 178). Again, these elements, appearing simultaneously, serve to reinforce the notion that the Modern paradigm is in serious jeopardy in Portugal. The emergence of competing thoughts about the literary trajectory of the country's writers, thus, reflects the Crisis Phase in a uniquely straight-forward manner. The fact that the same social and political, as well as intimate and individualistic, issues faced by the Portuguese of this era take shape in the literature simply strengthens this idea.

To conclude, we have seen how the Modern paradigm which has guided Portugal to the end of the first half of the Twentieth Century begins to break down in the beginning of the second half. According to Kuhn's theory of the Paradigm Shift, this social, political and literary breakdown and conscience toward the need for change and, indeed, for a new system, indicates that the Portugal is in a Crisis Phase. The proof of this has shown itself in the socio-political context which as lead to literary movements whose trajectories, although based in the historical legacy of the 1920s, 30s and 40s, (the generations of *Orpheu, Presença* and the Surrealist movement), break away from those forms to include foreign influences as well as open criticism of the existing political and social regimes.

In the next chapter we will see how the development of the Spanish state in the same period, approximately from 1955-1975, reveals striking similarities and differences to the process described in this chapter. We will be able to observe the same process, but with subtle differences in literary and social dynamics evolving out of the Crisis Phase there. All in all, nonetheless, these two distinct societies remain in competition with one another, yet growing ever more similar during the second half of the Twentieth Century.

# Chapter II: 1955 to 1975, Ángel González and José Hierro

In comparison with Portugal, Spain in the 1950s seems a unique form of exaggeration in all realms—the social, the political and the literary. While the conservative elements of the Franco regime still hold absolute power, the country enters an economic boom period in which, as in Portugal, foreign investment and influence begin to filter into the country. Unlike in Portugal, nonetheless, the regime seems to become even more defensive in terms of social control, while simultaneously seeming to lose ground to the artistic communities that criticize it. This could have to do with a characteristic that Pinedo has noticed of Spain as a nation which has seemingly opposed Modernity, preferring instead a more theologically-driven vision of the universe (Pinedo 41). Also, as we will see, there is not necessary an oligarchic social structure, but a military dictatorship in place. This means that the wealthy classes will not see the coming changes as a threat, at least not until the few years preceding the fall of the Franco regime. During this period a new generation of poets began writing in Spain, one whose members had survived the Civil War as children and grown up during the first decades of the dictatorship (Debicki 99). Their poetry appears in the 1950s as more socially-inclined, one of the few art forms which the censors permitted (Bau 397). In the 60s, due to industrial growth, the influence of foreign film and music, and the relative relaxing of censorship laws (Debicki 98), poetry expanded to include a less social and more metaphysical style (Bau 398). Two poets from this period who exemplify the transition are José Hierro and Ángel González.

Foreign influence on social change plays a much a similar role in Portugal. Spain, particularly in the 19th and 20th Centuries, was seen as "displaced to the periphery of the modern within the European imaginary (Iarocci xi)." In fact, it is the original destabilizing of the "putatively stable medieval culture" that caused the Modern paradigm's social and political Modernity and literary Renaissance within Europe, then later in Spain (4-5). Returning to the 20th Century, this foreign influence is enacted only with Franco's permission, as in every area "Franco maintained absolute power until his death in 1975 (Bou 397)." This holds true in several areas of Spanish (and Portuguese) societies, including the "corporate institutional structures [that] had a marginal and limited role, and reached stability thanks to the strategic parts played by Salazar and Franco. Both were final arbitrator . . . (Sapelli 77)."

Artistically speaking, the 1950s and 60s see the acceptance and diffusion of a new type of critical art. In theatre, Antonio Buero Vallejo's more subtle brand of social criticism becomes designated as "Posibilismo." "As Buero's prominence in the circles of Spanish theater grew, an understanding of this fusion of social criticism with the parameters of Francoist censorship emerged: *posibilismo*, or "possibilism", representing the idea of writing what was possible within the boundaries of what the censors would accept (Ladner 10)." At the same time, another dramaturge, Alfonso Sastre creates a philosophical approximation to censorship known as "Imposibilismo," negating the oblique style of Buero Vallejo by directly criticizing dictatorial, military regimes such as Franco's as dehumanizing. In fact, "[t]he word *posibilismo* was developed to represent the antithesis of Sastre's assertion that there was a perceived idea that an *imposibilismo* ("impossibilism") existed in the Spanish theater under Franco, based in the assumption that there existed certain taboos not to be addressed in works to be submitted to censors of the regime (10)." In the area of the novel one name remains above all others: Camilo José Cela. His obra magna, *La Colmena*, represents well the environment of horror, fear and loss of self-identification that defines 1950s Spanish society.

In poetry we also find two separate trajectories that are eerily similar to those of the Neo-Realists and Experimentalists (respectively) of Portugal. The first, represented by poets such as Claudio Rodríguez, Gloria Fuertes and Ángel González (in his very early work), defines itself as a socially-conscious poetry, particularly in connection with the latter two poets' "whose social and political *engagement* was overt (Miller 343)." Their works, as those of Buero Vallejo, Sastre and Cela, focus on social and political issues of the period as the raison d'être of literature. We will study the work of Ángel González in this period to examine more closely this idea, as well as how González breaks this mold, traversing what will come to be an introduction to the questioning of language's hermeneutic limitations.

On the other hand, there is a movement occurring parallel to the experimentalists in Portuguese poetry, but with a testimonial element which both expands on, and differs from, the experience of formal experimentalism which defines the Portuguese poetic scene of the era. This tendency, known as "la poesía testimonial," (Eng., "Testimonial Poetry") reveals the internalization of the poetic subject's experience in the Franco regime, not critically as in the social writers' works, but sensationally, as in the poetry of Herberto Helder [within the definition of "testimonial poets" I include the "novísimos" for their more intimate and simultaneously playful synchronic foci. This is particularly true in the works of Guillermo Carnero (Pritchett 125-126)]. The criticism is on a more individual basis, with the inclusion of historical perspectives insofar as they pertain to the realm of the individual experience, and not necessarily with the larger social well-being in mind. The poetry of José Hierro, as we will soon see, serves to define this other poetic experience in Spain.

Let us return to Ángel González, who begins his work in the 1950s and 60s as a both a socially aware and yet intimate poet, yet often expressing the limits of life and its dependence on language as its primary mode of expression (Debicki 114-115). His poetry of the 1950s may be noted for "verso de experiencia, vocabulario riguroso encuadrado en un tono de conversación, interés moral en el personaje protagonista de los poemas y . . . la geografía urbana (González, *101 + 19 = 120, 7*)." [Eng., "verse of experience, a rigorous vocabulary framed in a conversational tone, moral interest in the protagonist of the poems and . . . urban geography" (Translation by Robert Simon)]. González's poetic work continues to evolve into the 1970s and 80s (163), taking on topics such as the poetic subject's relationship with memory and aging, and a dialog with the concept of history within the confines of poetic language (Valero 2). His use of a plain and simpler language has been shown as revealing an intertextual relationship between his own text and that of Juan Ramón Jiménez, especially concerning the topic of death (Wilcox, "Ángel González," 37). In one of his most recent works, *Otoños y otras luces* (2001), González's poetic subject focuses entirely on the topics mentioned above while simultaneously adulating life, love and poetry's connection with both (2-3). His view of language also evolves, becoming more postmodern through a "tendency to self-referentiality and indeterminacy" that invites the reader to participate in the linguistic games played (165). In a poetic environment which slowly begins to welcome these tendencies, González challenges the notion of the "master narrative" through a questioning of the notion of absolute truth with which the reader enters into the text (Deters 239).

As an example of his work from the period following the social period, namely, from the 1950s, we see in *Áspero mundo* (1956) the following poem:

Para que yo me llame Ángel González,
para que mi ser pese sobre el suelo,
fue necesario un ancho espacio
y un largo tiempo:
hombres de todo mar y toda tierra,
fértiles vientres de mujer, y cuerpos
y más cuerpos, fundiéndose incesantes
en otro cuerpo nuevo.
Solsticios y equinoccios alumbraron
con su cambiante luz, su vario cielo,
el viaje milenario de mi carne
trepando por los siglos y los huesos.
De su pasaje lento y doloroso
de su huida hasta el fin, sobreviviendo
naufragios, aferrándose
al último suspiro de los muertos,
yo no soy más que el resultado, el fruto,
lo que queda, podrido, entre los restos;
esto que veis aquí,
tan sólo esto:
un escombro tenaz, que se resiste
a su ruina, que lucha contra el viento,
que avanza por caminos que no llevan
a ningún sitio. El éxito
de todos los fracasos. La enloquecida
fuerza del desaliento . . .

Aquí, Madrid, mil novecientos
cincuenta y cuatro: un hombre solo.

Un hombre lleno de febrero,
ávido de domingos luminosos,
caminando hacia marzo paso a paso,
hacia el marzo del viento y de los rojos
horizontes—y la reciente primavera
ya en la frontera del abril llovioso . . .—

Aquí, Madrid, entre tranvías
y reflejos, un hombre: un hombre solo.

—Más tarde vendrá mayo y luego junio,
y después julio y, al final, agosto —.

Un hombre con un año para nada
Delante de su hastío para todo.
    (González, *101 + 19 = 120*, 23-4)

(Eng. So that I may be called Ángel González,
so that my being may weigh above the floor,
a wide space was necessary
and a long time:
men from every sea and all the Earth,
women's fertile bellies, and bodies
and more bodies, incessantly fusing
into another new body.
Solstices y equinoxes glowed
with their changing light, their varied sky,
the thousand year voyage of my flesh
tripping through centuries and bones.
From their painful and slow passage
from the fleeing to the end, surviving
shipwrecks, grasping
at the last breaths of the dead,
I am no more than the result, the fruit,
what remains, rotted, among the rest;
this is what you see,
just this:
a tenacious rubble, that resists
its ruin, that fights against the wind,
that walks upon roads that do not take you
to anywhere. Success
of all the failures. The crazed
force of discouragement . . .

Here, Madrid, nineteen hundred
And fifty-four: a man alone.

A man full of February,
greedy for illuminated Sundays,
walking step by step toward March,
toward the March of wind and of red
horizons—and the recent Spring
already on the border with rainy April . . .—

Here, Madrid, between cable-cars
And reflections, a man: a man alone.

—Later May will come and then June,
and alter that July and, in the end, August —.

A man with a year for nothing
facing his disgust for everything.)

(translation by Robert Simon)

We may observe in this poem that, while the social focus is very much present, the metaphysical questions which will eventually dominate González' work have already begun to appear. The poem begins with the notion that all men are fusing into one, perhaps and allusion to the solidarity that a social poet would have wanted to reflect in his work. However, as the poem develops we observe a greater focus on the poetic subject himself and his very intimate existential crisis, placing himself then in a very specific and concrete exterior context. In this way the theme of solidarity is transformed into that of solitude within the greater context of mass solitude, on a societal scale. As García Montero points out, "Es el sentimiento personal de la soledad lo que se nombra. El poema expone el modo de vivir la soledad en un año y una ciudad concreta, en unas costumbres dibujadas. La poesía puede situarse precisamente en el punto de cruce y conexión que hay entre la experiencia del autor y del resto de los ciudadanos que viven la misma historia (González, *101 + 19 = 120*, 8)." [Eng., "It is the personal feeling of solitude that is named. The poem exposes solitude as a way of living in a concrete year and city, in certain pre-drawn customs. Poetry can place itself precisely in the point of crossing and connection that exists between the author's experience and the rest of the citizens that live the same story" (Translation by Robert Simon)].[6] Ironically, it is the specificity of the poetic subject's context in later stanzas that makes his situation that much less concrete and more abstractly related to the first stanza. Thus, even in this early stage of social preoccupations, the notions of existential crisis, the questioning of history's ability to define hermeneutically those living in it and the relationship between the intimate and its context all play a part in González' work.

José Hierro, a poet already known by 1950 for his testimonial poetry [in works such as *Tierra sin nosotros* (1947), *Alegría* (1947), and *Quinta del 42* (1952) (Soriano 22)], published *Cuánto sé de mí* in 1957 (Debicki 126). It is a work known for its combination of the older testimonial style with a newer, "subjective expression of the sense of loss" through which the poetic subject, conscious of his role as a poetic witness, views his world (126). Although Hierro's poetry does not reflect as varied an evolution as that of González, his poetry does mark a noticeable change from the social poetry of the 1950s to the more metaphysical (and, perhaps, experimentalist) poetry of the 1960s.

---

6. All further translations into English, unless otherwise noted, are by Robert Simon.

*Cuánto sé de mí* serves as just such a transitional marker. It in fact also introduces several themes that will become important in Iberian postmodern poetry in general. First, the subjectivity expressed by the poetic subject has been seen as directly tied to the notion of the limits of language representing the limits of the subject (Bermúdez 247), a central topic in Postmodernism. According to Bermúdez, this limitation may only be overcome through the death of the flesh, and thus of the body which requires language to describe it (247). Also, although musicality in poetry is an essential element of Lorca's work (Boggs 209), in Hierro it is seen as a method by which the poetic subject may transcend the confines of literature, time and space (209). Finally, according to Luce López-Baralt, whose work on Iberian Mysticism is central to the argument for a Sufi influence in Iberian poetry, there is an intertextual presence of San Juan de la Cruz's (and, thus, the Iberian Sufi mystic Ibn 'Arabi's) mystical work in Hierro's poetry (López-Baralt 111). (This connection will become that much clearer when we delve into the mystical postmodern poetry of Clara Janés and Joaquim Pessoa in the final chapter of this study). It is important to note that a large part of Hierro's work is focused on the notion of transcendence, rather than on deconstruction or decentralization. Thus, even though his work is not postmodern, the subjectivity with which he testifies to the state of the world, as well as a constant desire for transcendence and the notion of death as an escape from the limitations of expression, will greatly influence Iberian Postmodernism.

In *Cuánto sé de mí* we see various examples of these techniques, such as in the poem "Criaturas de la sombra":

No podré nunca desencarcelaros,
maravillosos que abrasáis mi boca.
Dedos de luz, hundidos en la roca,
de vuestro rico mineral avaros.

Libertaros: nombraros. Libertaros:
mataros . . . Vuestro fuego desemboca
en mi garganta, mata cuanto toca,
muere – morís – bajo los cielos claros.

Maravillosos de la sombra. Sones
otorgadores de secretos dones,
a silencios perpetuos os sentencio,

a vivir, prisioneros, siempre a oscuras.
(Silencio.) Impronunciables criaturas
que no (silencio) . . . naceréis. (Silencio.)

(Hierro 63)

(Eng. 'Tis you I shan't from jail let out,
the marvelous ones who burn my lips.
Fingers of light, from your mineral rich
Avid, and in the rock most sunk.

To free you: to name you. To free you:
to kill you . . . your fire empties out
in my throat, whatever it meets it puts out,
it dies – you die – under the skies sure.

The marvelous ones of shadow. Dins
The grantors of secret gifts,
I sentence you to perpetual silence,

to live, prisoners, where dark outstretches.
(Silence.) Unspeakable wretches
that will not (silence) . . . be born. (Silence.)
        (Translation by Robert Simon)

The form of this poem is that of a Petrarchian sonnet, creating a clear connection to more traditional poetic themes (which, ironically, are not present in the poem except to reinforce the principle theme of language's purposeful silence). The controlled sonnet form does not lend itself to the flexibility offered by free verse, "redondillas" or other popular poetic forms. Thus, the use of the sonnet both limits the poetic word (in theory) physically as well as thematically. However, we may observe that the use of enjambment, various intraverse breaks such as parentheticals, ellipsis and other stopping techniques create a unique and unexpected flow within the poem.

This uniqueness holds thematically as well as formally. For example, in the first stanza the theme of the poetic word as light trapped in darkness appears in Iberian mystical writings as an essential binary opposition representing metaphorically the duality of the mundane and divine (Simon, *Understanding*, 84). However, this theme functions solely as part of the freeing of poetic words, or poetic language, in the wider scope. Thus, even in the first stanza we see the reapplication of more traditional themes within the larger questioning of notions taken for granted throughout the Modern period (in this case, the question of the poetic word's absolute meaning and indisputable power). The second stanza reveals a similar reapplication—the notion of naming, or identifying, and thus killing, the poetic word harkens back to the same binary oppositions, while describing the need to question the essential nature of that word as somehow dangerous. The final two stanzas, the place of resolution in the Petrarchian sonnet, is actually the place where the poetic subject makes the decision to keep imprisoned the poetic word, leaving it unspoken and, thus, its homicidal power untouched. The "creatures of shadow," then, begin and remain the poetic word, powerful yet useless as such in a new poetic context.

In terms of the Paradigm Shift theory, Hierro's work exemplifies a moment of crisis, where, although one paradigm is still in effect, it no longer serves the purpose of expressing the experience of the present moment. Social poetry, although useful in the first two decades of the post-war era in Spain, does not reflect the situation in the late 50s and early 60s, where a new reality begins to take hold in the country. Thus, the emergence of a metaphysical strain in this period, such as that found in Hierro's poetry, finds its explanation as a symptom of the Crisis Phase.

The poetry of Ángel González, through a subjective, indeterminate language that questions absolute notions and forces the reader into an ambiguous (and somewhat decentralized) state in whose creation s/he has participated, reflects a moment in which a new paradigm, one of many competing paradigms in the Spanish context, begins to appear. This period in the shift, happening around the time of Franco's death and seen reflected in the poetry analyzed above, is recognizable as the Transitional Phase according to Kuhn's theories. The Modern paradigm is no longer in play – rather, we observe through poetic work that there are other conceptualizations of reality taking hold.

As in Portugal, the 1950s and 1960s reveal that the Crisis Phase of Modern Paradigm is in effect, with the trappings of the Transitional Phase visible. This paradigm no longer able to define the new changes in Spain and still serve the ends of what have become the more traditionalist elements that feed into the Franco regime's socio-religious philosophies. The result is a divide among representative works in the period: those who espouse an attitude of critical desperation, namely the social poets, and those who create an intimate poetic of fragmentation, namely the testimonial poets. In is important to note that for the social poets, whose work moves away from (or beyond, depending on your point of view) fragmentation, there exists a movement toward the desire for social freedom.

Thus, the division is set between the social vs. the intimate poetries of the period. This clear difference indicates that there may now be two possibilities that represent challenges within Spain to the defunct Modern paradigm.

We should recognize, then, the difference between this process in Portugal and its counterpart process in Spain. Although present, the foreign influence that we have so discussed and analysed in Portuguese poetry, and thus Portuguese culture, is relatively minimal in Spanish poetry of the period. It seems as though the poets in Spain desire to find a resolution that is absolutely Spanish in nature, and, thus, counters the essentially external, and thus Modern, paradigm's influence. The desire, then, is similar to that of the Portuguese poets studied here, but with a more internal focus that the Portuguese, who accept the up and coming poetic forms and techniques from abroad more readily. Also, due to the Spanish government dealing more harshly with alternative opinions to those of the Franco regime's socio-political philosophy, the "small rebellions" so important in the relationship between Portuguese poets and Spanish ones seem more controlled and subtle. We see that when the attacks are more direct, the Spanish government simply shuts down the artist, in both venue and person, as seen in the example of Sastre's dramatic work in the 1940s and 50s. "Although Sastre was successful in publishing numerous articles in the area of theory and was able to oversee the production of some of his plays, he remained largely silenced as a playwright under the Franco regime due to the political content of his works, with many of his best dramas never being viewed in Spain during the course of the dictatorship (Ladner 22-3)." Thus, fewer voices speak out against the Spanish regime, while in Portugal it seems almost in vogue to criticize the government through literary practices.

Yet, it is through the theory of the Paradigm Shift itself that we find the overpowering similarities between the two cases, at least through the early 1970s when the Iberian dictatorships have begun their rapid decline and eventual fall (in Portugal in 1974, and in Spain in 1975). It is clear that the Modern paradigm in both Portuguese and Spanish societies has entered into the Crisis Phase, and perhaps even begun the competition of possible future paradigms which defines the Transition Phase. The questioning of the Modern paradigm as competent to define and encapsulate the new world being born in these two countries reveals itself through the poetry studied in this and the previous chapter. The appearance of competing voices to represent this era in poetry, then, reflects the competing voices in the socio-political spectrum of these societies. In other words, the dissention and movement of the working classes, the governments' inability, in each case, to keep the kind of control in either the arena of politics (as in Portugal) or that of economic growth and its relationship to social and artistic change (as in Spain) become evident.

In conclusion, we may observe that, on the one hand, there are similarities in the presence of an evident literary reaction to dictatorial governments whose power base, for one reason or another, is weakening. On the other, these reactions change according to the context in which they occur. This makes logical sense, given the differences in the contexts through which each process happens. In any case, the Crisis Phase of the period of approximately 1950 to 1975 in Iberia will give way to a Transitional Phase of competing paradigms in the late 1970s and the 1980s, whose voices in poetry are as diverse and rich as those of the period before. In the next chapter we will see two of the primary competing voices at the turn of the government in Portugal, one extending from the Neo-Realist line, the other, a perspective on the essential whose writing could almost be postmodern.

# Chapter III: 1974 to 1990, Ruy Belo and Vasco Graça Moura

As we have seen in the previous two chapters, the period of approximately 1950 to 1974-5 marks a distinct Crisis Phase in the Paradigm Shift that will bring Spain and Portugal ever closer to a new socio-political, and thus literary, paradigm. The Modern paradigm has lead to the dictatorships that rule both countries. We have observed that it begins to break down as the economic stresses on the social and political systems that allow for oligarchic and military control (in Portugal and Spain, respectively) are no longer suited to handle the change. Disenchanted working classes in Portugal and more mobile working classes in Spain challenge the older, locally-based governance system as the economy becomes evermore industrialized. Particularly in Portugal, the Colonial Wars have devastated the rural population and brought criticism against the government for its inflexible colonial policies.

In terms of poetry, different and competing groups of writers form as the social, political and intimately personal dynamics begin playing out in Iberian society. Two main groups form, however, that reflect the major forces at work in Spanish and Portuguese societies: the social poets, concerning with the larger issues of government and societal woes; and the more intimate poets, whose experiments in form and theme lead to an analysis of the individual's experience in this new world. Each group represents the possibility for a new paradigm, yet neither seems to take a dominant stance. This phenomenon signals, according to Kuhn's theory, the coming of the Transitional Phase. The saga continues, as we will see in this chapter, with the social seeming to meld into the intimate, a good sign of artistic postmodernism, although not so perfectly so to defend the notion that the Transitional Phase would by then be complete (with social Postmodernity, and thus, literary postmodernism, the supposed winners).

We shall now return to the appearance of postmodernism in Portuguese poetry. Its development in Portugal may be recognized specifically during the period of 1970-2000. The beginning of the post-dictatorship era marked a moment of recognition within the country that she was lagging both socially and artistically (Seixo 406). Postmodernism's presence, then, marks a change in the perception of Portugal as no longer belonging only to the past (Bou 402).

In many ways the Portuguese live in a combined world of traditional culture, propagandized during the country's dictatorship period, and of the international culture of the European Union, a newly opened free-market economy and cultural postmodernity (Kaufman 17). Interestingly, Spanish exploitation of the lower wages in Portugal has created an economic quasi-colonialism rivaled only by that of the British during the 17th, 18th and 19th Centuries (Birmingham 191). This phenomenon, along with the slow development of industry and disillusionment with the democratic government's ability to lead the people out of their misery, turned the populace from highly optimistic in the 1970s (Kaufman 16) to somewhat doubtful, in the 1980s, that change was possible (18-19). The questioning of traditional artistic modes, such as Neo-Realism, and the rejection of modes of expression such as "Fado" by the populace (Birmingham 179), allow the entering into the country of a more effective means of expressing a more modern Portuguese culture (Kaufman 18). Thus, the realization of an uncertain future in the 1980s and 90s (Seixo 406), fueled by an ambiguous cultural, political and social status both within and without [summed up in Sousa Santos' declaration that Portugal is a "semi-peripheral" nation (Santos 58)], has become the background for the development of postmodernism in Portuguese poetry.

The process of the adoption of postmodernism in Portuguese arts seems to fit within the social process described above. There is a more sudden swing from the essentially Modernist, Surrealist and Neo-Realist tendencies of the period of the "presencistas," roughly between 1920 and 1950, to the appearance of postmodernism as an artistic element or set of techniques in the 1970s.[7] This could be an entirely artistic phenomenon, as according to Marinho, the plurality of voices heard in Portuguese poetry in the 1960s reflects the failure of the poetic word as an efficient and useful tool for expressing meaning and universality. " . . . os anos 60,

---

7. I remind the reader that it is evident, as stated in the introduction to this study, that the debate about postmodernism as a break from "Modernism" or as simply another, acerbic, phase of it (Cruz 216) still exists in Portuguese criticism.

profundamente [influenciados] pela crise dos valores sociais, apostam na recusa do sentido, vivendo angustiadamente a inutilidade da palavra e a sua terrível ineficácia . . ." (Marinho 41). (Eng. "The 1960s, profoundly influenced by the crisis in social values, put their money on the escape from feeling, living anxiously the non-utility of the [poetic] word and its terrible inefficacy"). Even for those who doubt the usefulness of such as all-encompassing term like "postmodernism," the movement toward "uma nova consciência histórica" (Amaral 24) (Eng. "a new historical consciousness") is undeniable. In any case, and no matter what the catalyst, this process, rather stunning relative to what seems a more measured development of postmodernism in neighboring Spain, began toward the end of the 1950s and continued on to the adoption of postmodernism as present and strongly felt in Portuguese poetry in the 1990s. It also kept firm to the surrealist symbolism inherited from poets such as Mário Cesariny, incorporating a questioning of the notion of memory, as both a rebellion against the principles of the modernist "master narrative" and as a basis for the opening up to the postmodern ideals of decentralization and deconstruction.

As stated above, postmodernism in Portuguese art is characterized by the deconstruction, decentralization, irony, and relativism seen at the beginning of this study. Its uniqueness, however, come from its so-called "revivalism." "Daí as citações, o intencional regresso a formas historicamente definidas, o ecletismo, a convocação de estilos polifonicamente diversificados e entrosados que hão-de permitir que se fale de um novo-romantismo . . . de novo-simbolismo, de novo-expressionismo, de novo-surrealismo abjeccionista, etc., para não falarmos antes de uma figura que poderá ser comum a todas estas formas de *revival* e que é precisamente a da paródia ou a da ironia" (Guimarães, *A Poesia Contemporânea*, 172) (Eng., "And from there the citations, the intentional return to historically defined forms, the eclectic, the invoking of diversified, polyphonic and integrated styles which much permit speaking of a new Romanticism . . . a new Symbolism, a new Expressionism, a new Abject Surrealism, etc., without even mentioning the figure to be common to all of these *revivalist* forms, necessarily that of parody or that of irony"). The postmodern of Portuguese literary arts is a polyfaceted series of intertextual games played, in some writers, with recently past poetic movements, such as in the case of João Manuel Magalhães' poetic dialogue with the work of the mid Twentieth-Century poet Carlos de Oliveira (Gusmão 171), or as that of Ruy Belo, whose inferences to, and dialogue with, poets such as Fernando Pessoa and Bocage (Cruz 111). In other writers, such as Vasco Graça Moura (as will be seen below), there is a constantly evolving intertextual relationship between traditional and popular styles, along with much older poets and poetic styles, such as that of the Renaissance poet Camões. Finally, there exist also the writings of Nuno Júdice, whose "discursive and visionary exuberance found likewise in Herberto Helder" (Gusmão 172) set him apart from the others in his intertextual dialogue with a 1960s experimentalist discourse. This connection with both the recent and distant past, with a particular focus on imperial-era discourse, is thus one of the most distinctive markers of Portuguese postmodernism and one which distinguishes it from other European postmodern tendencies.[8]

Although Ruy Belo lived only until 1978, his poetry has exercised an important influence on the postmodern works of the 1980s and 90s. One of the more apparent influences in Belo's poetry is that of the Surrealists of the 1940s. This will give his work a distinctive symbolic value to the poetic word (Guimarães, *A Poesia Contemporânea*, 77). However, "[esa] poesia está não só marcada pela valorização simbólica da linguagem poética, o que leva a realçar, no poema, a metáfora e a imagem, mas também pela sua configuração expressivamente significativa, o que conduz à valorização na sua superfície de certos núcleos semânticos (Guimarães, *A Poesia*, 78)." [Eng., " . . . this poetry is not only marked by the symbolic valuing of poetic language, which ends up emphasizing, in the poem, metaphor and image, but also by its expressively significant configuration, which drives toward the valuing of the surface of certain semantic nuclei" (Translation by Robert Simon)]. Beyond this combined Surrealist and existentialist poetry lies another aspect, that of "as preocupações que se enraízam numa dimensão humana . . . e que podem transformar-se, por sucessivas mediações de natureza verbal, em consciência de uma imagem do mundo ou de uma visão colectiva (79)." [Eng., "the worries that become rooted in a human dimension . . . and that may transform, through successive mediations of a verbal nature, in the conceptualization of an image of the world or of a collective vision" (Translation by Robert Simon)]. As Belo himself has stated:

---

8. Of course, other tendencies such as a focus on the discourse of the marginalized, including women, immigrants, etc., also plays an important role in postmodern Portuguese arts. For the purpose of this study, however, I have chosen to focus on "revivalism" as the primary characteristic. See Seixo, Maria-Alzira. "Postmodernism in Portugal." *International Postmodernism: Theory and Literary Practice*. Ed. Hans Bertens and Douwe Fokkema. Amsterdam: John Benjamins Publishing Company; 1997. pp. 405-410, for more information.

A solidão será porventura um problema burguês. Mas, numa sociedade onde todos os intelectuais mais ou menos o são, ela será talvez, numa perspectiva realista, não tanto o reflexo como a denúncia dessa mesma sociedade . . .
(Belo, *Obra*, 13)

(Eng., "Solidarity will be essentially a bourgeois problem. However, in a society where all intellectuals are more or less that, it will perhaps be, from a realist perspective, not so much a reflection but an accusation of that same society . . . ")
(Translation by Robert Simon)

So, while Belo's poetry does not necessarily take a politically-motivated vision of the poetic word, such as that which we would find in the Neo-Realist poetic (Guimarães, *A Poesia Contemporânea,* 79), we do see an unexpected combination of the Neo-Realist *social* preoccupations with the Experimentalists' desire for freedom from the nucleic semantic that defines the poetry written under the Modern paradigm.

An excellent example of this combination may be found in the poem "E Tudo Era Possível" from his collection, *Palavras de Tempo* (1969), the section titled "Primavera":

Na minha juventude antes de ter saído
da casa de meus pais disposto a viajar
eu conhecia já o rebentar do mar
das páginas dos livros que já tinha lido

Chegava o mês de maio era tudo florido
o rolo das manhãs punha-se a circular
e era só ouvir o sonhador falar
da vida como se ela houvesse acontecido

E tudo se passava numa outra vida
e havia para as coisas sempre uma saída
Quando foi isso? Eu próprio não o sei dizer

Só sei que tinha o poder duma criança
entre as coisas e mim havia vizinhança
e tudo era possível era só querer
(Belo, *Obra*, 171)

(Eng.,
When I was still young before I left home
ready to travel around in the world
I already knew about the waves' breaking
from the pages of all the books I'd read

When may rolled around everything was flowers
the morning turtledove flew here flew there
and to hear the dreamer just speak of life
was like it having actually happened

Everything took place in another life
and there was always a way out when needed
When was all this? Not even I can say

I know only that I had a child's power
all things were close to me and everything
was possible I only had to want it
        (Translation by Richard Zenith)

On the surface the poem seems a simple narration of the spirit and affirmation of youth's wonder and potential. By delving into the themes and poetic techniques, however, we will see the presence of the Surrealist and experimentalist visions, beyond the evident and personal realism of the poem.

The poem is written in the form of a Petrarchan sonnet, lending to the notion of something traditional and venerable, immobile in time and space. The form, thus, feeds the superficial theme described above. Nonetheless, the image of book pages in the first stanza as the emitters of water, a recognizable symbol of the meeting of the origin (from Kristeva's notion of the "chora") with the sea's interlocutor, or the poetic subject, creates a Surrealist scene reminiscent of those found in the work of Mário Cesariny or Alexandre O'Neill. It also places the poetic subject in the position of interpreter of the work to the poem's reader. We see this in the second stanza, when we see the connection made between the dove (a symbol of the soul in mystical and religious poetry), the dreamer (assumedly the poetic subject himself) and the combination of the Surrealist dream-world with the reality that this dream-world has seemingly transformed into something more like itself. Of course, this creates the conflict which the quartets of the sonnet form requires, that of the tension between the poetic subject as reader / writer of his world, and as subjected to a "real" world which, in his mind, takes second place. It is in the tercets, then, that we see the supposed resolution. The poetic subject, on the surface, has defaulted to the cliché of the child's imagination surviving the world; I do not, however, see that the poet stops there. The duality between the two "lives" of the poetic subject is conserved, meaning that the existential crisis of the Surrealist dream-state versus the mundane reality that it belies is accepted. (This acceptance of the notion of an uncentered universe will eventually be a catalyst for the literary postmodernism that Moura embodies later on.) These novel combinations also make sense from the Experimentalist perspective, as they are precisely the type of thematic that, in such an intimate and personal context, reflects the innovations appearing at the time.

Vasco Graça Moura has become emblematic of both postmodernism in contemporary Portuguese poetry and the effect of Postmodernity on an individual's career. Both his artistic and political life have reflected a sense of movement from one genre to another, from poetry to theatre, novels and essay on the one hand, and on the other, from extreme leftist during the revolutionary period to holding a position in the contemporary government of Portugal (Oliveira, "Biobibliografia," 32).[9] In terms of his poetry, although seemingly pertaining to the same neo-Surrealist strain as Helder's, it actually forms part of an intertextualization of the Surreal with Renaissance symbolism and thematics (Lancastre 36). This allows the poetic subject in Moura's poetry to explore the theme of memory as an intertextual game played between past and present that both draws out the omni-presence of the former in the latter and reveals the chaos lurking underneath a seemingly stable poetic tradition:

> "O fantástico, o real, a «self-reflexivity» e a citação [of works from 16th Century Renaissance poetry], são as quatro constantes através das quais o poeta age para enredar e ao mesmo tempo destabilizar o seu leitor. Porque estas quatro constantes, assim combinadas, criam equivocidade e ironia, abrem, embora no respeito quase férreo da tradição métrica, para um novo universo: um caos que se esconde por entre as malhas apertadas da observância tradicional, e que é constituído pelo *assemblage*" (Lancastre 36).

> (Eng. "The fantastic, the real, «self-reflexivity» and citation . . . , are the four constants by the way of which the poet acts to entangle and at the same time destabilize the reader. Because the four constants, combined as such, create error and irony, they open, although almost in iron respect to metric tradition, to a new universe: a chaos that hides itself between the tight mesh of traditional observance and that is constituted in an *assemblage*.") (Translation by Robert Simon)

The presence of music (along with the inherent musicality) in many works, such as *Letras do Fado Vulgar* (2001), adds to this enigmatic and ironic mix (Andrade 43). In fact, the postmodern game of anachronisms becomes plain in his recycling of "Fado" in intertextually rich poems such as "conhecimento:"

---

9. It should be noted that Oliveira's original term "government Propaganda Office," has been avoided here due to its derogatory connotation.

fiz no teu corpo à noite a travessia
de mares e céus e terras e vulcões
e em breve rodopio as estações
detinham-se esquecidas e foi dia

a memória das praias e florestas
perpassou-me na pele e entranhou-se
como um suave afago que assim fosse
espuma que ficou de iras honestas

e ao despertar de tanta sonolência
formou-se devagar esta canção
para entreter de novo o coração
tão paciente em sua impaciência

até que sendo noite eu atravesso
uma outra vez o mundo, o mar, o vento.
amar é sempre mais conhecimento
e conhecer é tudo o que eu te peço.
        (Moura, *Letras do Fado Vulgar*, 42)

(Eng.
In your evening body a voyage I made
of seas and skies, volcano and earth
and the stations in a quick turn
would remain forgotten and it was day

the memory of beaches and of trees
through my skin it slipped and raveled
as a soft caress as if it were
foam that remained of virtuous spleen.

and on waking from such sleep
this song was slowly formed
to entertain again the heart
so patient in its pique

until it being night I cross
once more the sea, the wind, the world.
Love is always more to know,
and knowing is all that of you I call.)
        (Translation by Robert Simon)

There are, of course, certain rhythmic and symbolic points in this poem which are both common to any "fado" tune as well as the first poetries of the modern period in Portugal. In terms of the rhythm, the use of the hendecasyllabic, four-verse ABBA rhyme-scheme, known as octave, was commonly utilized by the poets of the Renaissance Period both by itself (as reflected above) and in conjunction with the sestet for the reproduction of the Petrarchan Sonnet form. In fact, the dedication of the poem is the third verse from the following stanza by Camões in his *Lusíadas*:

> Oh, que famintos beijos na floresta,
> E que mimoso choro que soava!
> Que afagos tão suaves! Que ira honesta,
> Que em risinhos alegres se tornava!
> O que mais passam na manhã e na sesta,
> Que Vénus com prazeres inflamava,
> Milhor é exprimentá-lo que julgá-lo;
> Mas julgue-o quem não pode exprimentá-lo.
> (Camões, *Os Lusíadas*, Canto IX, 313, Stanza 83)

> (Eng.: What ravenous kisses filled the wood!
> What little moans and tender weeping!
> What sweet caresses! What virtuous anger,
> Yielding to happy, compliant laughter!
> What further happened that morn and noon
> As Venus fanned the flames of love,
> Better to relish than disparage it;
> Let those begrudge who cannot manage it.)
> (White 193)

Although this particular stanza does not follow the rhyme-scheme found in Moura's poem, the stanza has great relevance for the analysis of it. This scene occurs during the time in which Vasco da Gama's crew has found the Island of Love, or the "Ilha dos Amores," and is enjoying a respite with the sexually-oriented nymphs present. The stanza serves to outline the pleasures the island provides and to inform the reader that the promiscuity described should not be judged harshly, although the narrator knows that the jealous will judge. In any case, this stanza has also appeared as the lyrics of a fado tune performed by Cristina Branco.[10] So, immediately the intertextual presence of both Renaissance poetry and "fado" lyric are felt in the poem.

Returning to Moura's poem, the greatest difference between the two is that while the original (i.e., Camões' *Os Lusíadas*) is part of a larger

---

10. As I plan to show in future studies and using this example, there exists a clear symbiotic relationship between fado and poetry in contemporary Portugal. This dialectic, characterized by mutual permission for agency of voice, as well as mutual subjectivity, by each of the other, functions for the survival and distribution (ironically extra-nationally) of both artistic modes.

work which exalts the Portuguese colonizing subject, the more recent version of the story is a more intimate exploration of the sailor's true desires. It links his travels with the experience of the island in terms of the nostalgic remembrance of the places visited, rather than as a series of national victories. Also, and just as importantly, Moura's at the poem's end the poetic subject states that "love is always more knowledge / and knowledge is all that I ask of you." The physical act of sex, then, takes a less important role – that of the type of memory found in "fado" music, that of a nostalgic looking-back to the past, is the pleasure which "entranhou-se / como um suave afago que assim fosse / espuma que ficou de iras honestas." The ironic switching of physical love with nostalgia in the poem follows Moura's deconstructive style. In other words, he has utilized the same language of the pro-imperialist and nationalist *Lusíadas* to subvert its original message and "vulgarize" it, first undermining its essentialist discourse and then including it intertextually within the both popular and widely rejected discourse (as seen above in my short explanation of Portuguese cultural evolution) of a common "fado" tune.

Beyond the combining of Surrealism, 16th Century Lyric and "Fado" lurks yet another element, the quotidian, which Moura represents as the anecdotal "vulgaridade de situações" (Eng. "vulgarity of situations") in his poetry (Moura 9-10). As becomes evident in collections such as *A Sequência da Baleia*, and *Concerto Campestre* (1993), the notion of the quotidian as anecdotal is not limited to simple, day-to-day happenings, but may include an ironic carnivalizing of the way the media transform the simple into the hyperbolic. For example, *A Sequência da Baleia ("o caso flácido da baleia moretal que deu à costa perto da póvoa do varzim)* is a ludic and critical look at an "episódio de um passado muito recente que os jornais, as televisões e as rádios que temos elevaram ao estátuto de catástrofe planetária" (Blanco 41). (Eng. "episode from a very recent past that our newspapers, TVs and radios elevated to the status of a planetary catastrophe"). This insertion of the real and "circunstancial" (Guimarães, *A Poesia Contemporânea*, 117) into a critically deconstructive poetic discourse opens a space for cultural action (Matos 45), perhaps stemming from his political and social leanings as mentioned above, and thus for a "healthy" provocation of the reader (Blanco 42). The deconstructive, and thus postmodern, aspect of undermining the notions behind that which may be seen as quotidian is evident. Moura's intertextual combination of the present (and, thus, "real") with the past (as seen in his use of 17th Century poetic meters) also reinforces the all-important notions of irony (Guimarães 116-117) and ambiguity (Navarro

43) which form the basis of Derrida's "différance" and, thus, the exist-ence of postmodernism in Portugal.

The poetry of Ruy Belo and that of Vasco Graça Moura, in differing ways, reveals that the Paradigm Shift, according to Kuhn's theory, is in the Transitional Phase. Each continues one of the paths drawn out by either the Neo-Realist or the Experimentalist poets. Belo's work follows a more intimate path, although always aware of the poetic word's social function, while Moura's poetry takes on a more explicitly socio-political tone. Moura also unites the experimentalist experience with the post-modern one, a similar combination of techniques as that found in Hel-der's work but less individualized. In any case, we observe in each poet's work that the traditionalist style, a trait of the Neo-Realists of the 1950s and 60s, has given way to a competition between what we may call Be-lo's intimate Experimentalism (also visible in the works of poets such as Mário Cláudio) versus the social postmodernism of Moura (a poetry sim-ilar to that of Joaquim Pessoa, who we will study in a subsequent chap-ter). Thus, we are plainly within a Transitional Phase whose paradigms, reflected in poetry, have begun to coalesce with outside influences in an entirely non-traditional, deconstructionist discourse. It seems, then, that in Portuguese society and letters we may observe a general trend toward the Postmodern paradigm as that which has evolved into a dominating stance over the divisions which have come to define the Portuguese con-text in the decades previous. In this way, the battle within poetry reveals both the dramatic social and political change from dictatorship to democ-racy occurring in Portugal, as well as the competing notions of who the Portuguese should be as they and their nation draw ever more near to the Twenty-First Century. As we will see in the next chapter, the poetry of Spain, while representing a similar social and political battle, will (somewhat ironically) become relatively more open to postmodernism and deconstruction more readily, while simultaneously dealing with the strong traditions that attempt to bind the competing factions of Spanish society together.

# Chapter IV: 1980-2000, Ana Rossetti and Belén Gopegui

This study so far has focused on societies whose members, and particularly whose writers, have set in motion a grandiose change from one paradigm to the next. The older, Modern paradigm has not been able to foment a sufficient understanding of the political, economic, artistic, and social pressures, influences, and changes from both within and without. It has then been forced to succumb to newer concepts. These concepts, in competition with one-another, seem to have developed certain commonalities, such as an acceptance of what many would deem to be "postmodern" ideals (in both society and literature), despite the obvious differences in focus. Thus, this chapter will treat this social postmodernity and literary postmodernism as the results of a possible Postmodern paradigm, not just within the scope of poetry or politics, but as its own overreaching set of concepts and assertions that, according to Kuhn's theory, allow for the establishment of the new dominant paradigm. In conjunction with Chapter V, it will also begin to tackle the important question of Iberia's position within the Paradigm Shift, revealing whether these societies have surpassed the Transitional Phase and adopted a new paradigm or not.

Between 1974 and 1975 both Spain and Portugal had seen their dictatorships fall. The development of postmodernism in Spanish poetry, specifically during the period of 1970-2000, marks a change in the perception of Iberian cultures as no longer belonging entirely to the past (Bou 402). The Franco dictatorship which ruled Spain for most of the Twentieth Century had been replaced as of 1975. In fact, Franco's death on 21 November, 1975 (Hooper 29), marked the end of a period of economic growth known as the "años de desarrollo," in which Spain developed from a rural and relatively impoverished country to become the world's ninth greatest industrial power (18). This unprecedented economic growth was due to a combination of high levels of importation and a constant flow of tourist dollars during the 1960s and early 70s, along with foreign investment in the country (19). Unlike what happened in Portugal, the Spanish government welcomed all of these income-attracting economic and developmental decisions (19-20). Although corruption and social stratification abounded (21), the country saw a level of prosperity unheard of in the years prior to the Civil War. By the approval of the first post-Franco democratic constitution in 1977, however, the 'economic miracle' had ended and prosperity had begun to decline (25-28). It had also become evident that, despite the increase in personal wealth that all Spaniards enjoyed, the division of wealth among the social classes had not changed (27). So, with the death of Franco and the rise of the Partido Socialista Obrero Español in the late 1970s and early 1980s, or the Spanish Socialist Party, there appeared a chance for renewed economic growth as well as a more egalitarian distribution of wealth in Spain (52-53). However, as the 1980s moved to a close it became clear that the Socialist Party would not attempt to change the uneven distribution of wealth in the country (61), one of many reasons for which the more conservative Partido Popular, or Popular Party, began taking more and more parliamentary seats during the 1980s and 90s (62-69). In fact, social critics have commented on an important aspect of the transition period that differentiates it from that of other countries, namely, the control maintained by the ruling class over the transition to democracy (López 36). The Spanish case is, thus, one of a transition "from above" (Kaufman 13).

Culturally, the Spanish (both Castilian and non-Castilian in their cultural identity) have begun to accept its linguistic and national plurality while simultaneously maintaining a unified, central government (Hooper 371). These contradictory systems, however, have come with much difficulty. "Negotiations between the central [Castilian] and the peripheral [Galician, Catalan and Basque nations] have not been easy (Sapelli 182)." The people's adherence to the church, an essential element of Spanish culture in the previous period of Modernity, began to wane during the post-Franco era (133). This was due in part to a secularization of the general populace, especially those born at or after the transition period (133-4). The generally conservative nature of the Spanish clergy came into sharp contrast with the more liberal political culture of the 1980s and 90s, a fact made plain through a "virtual absence of ideology from Spanish politics" (143). In this seemingly anti-clerical situation, however, there is still a strong sentiment that Catholicism serves as an element of national identity (126). It is in this disillusioned and complex moral and political situation that the set of deconstructive and decentralizing principles that guide literary postmodernism become explicit and seem to take hold in Spain.

From this point on, then, we will devote our time to the analysis of works by several "postmodern" poets in Spain and Portugal whose presence reflects literary postmodernism as defined in the Introduction to this study, but how also bring about older literary movements as part of their own self-deconstruction. It is here that we are forced to ask ourselves if what we have considered the Postmodern paradigm is truly the ruling paradigm in peninsular cultures, or if these cultures are still in what Kuhn would call their "Transitional Phase." We will begin with the poetics of Ana Rossetti, a clearly postmodern, Spanish poet from the government backed artistic movement known as the *movida* in Madrid, then move on to the work of Belén Gopegui's poetic prose, finishing our study in the next chapter with sample poems by two of the more intriguing poets in Contemporary Iberian letters, Clara Janés and Joaquim Pessoa.

Ana Rossetti, born in 1950, grew up during a period of relatively relaxed censorship and came of age in an historical period marked, as explained above, by, as Debicki states, "a lack of historical perspective, uncertainty regarding the future" (179). Her ironic undermining of cultural "master narratives" concerning the phallocentric through carefully utilized sexual imagery (211-212) allows for a deconstruction (through carnavalasque inversion) of a culture of male-dominated hegemony (213). Her work *Indicios vehementes* (1985) is one that many consider one of her most telling works, in which in poems such as "Chico Wrangler," the inversion of the male-female, or dominant-submissive, relationship function in the context of a foreign advertisement (Debicki 213 and Ferradáns 25):

Dulce corazón mío de súbito asaltado.
Todo por adorar más de lo permisible.
Todo porque un cigarro se asienta en una boca
y en sus jugosas sedas se humedece.
Porque una camiseta incitante señala
de su pecho, el escudo durísimo,
y un vigoroso brazo de la mínima manga sobresale.
Todo porque unas piernas, unas perfectas piernas,
Dentro del más ceñido pantalón, frente a mí se separan.
Se separan.
      (Rossetti 99)

(Eng., "Mine sweet heart suddenly robbed.

All to adore more than is permitted.
All because a cigarette sits in a mouth
and moistens in its juicy silks.
Because an enticing shirt signals
from his chest, a very hard shield,
and a vigorous arm overcomes the shortest sleeve.
All because some legs, some perfect legs,
Inside of the tightest pant, facing me, separate.
Separate.")
        (Translation by Robert Simon)

In this single-stanza poem, the inversion of the male hegemony mentioned above is evident. The application of additional aesthetic meaning to a popular object whose purpose is entirely commercial (that is, to gain customers and make money) indicates another, very postmodern aspect of Rossetti's work, the marking of an absence of universal meaning (Moreiras Menor 108). Her work also demonstrates the emphasis on Spanish culture as having become one of the "spectacle," where one searches out appearances but not meaning (108). Decentralization occurs, thus, through the deconstruction of ultimately superficial and vacuous cultural icons, such as an advertisement for pants, as indicative of a superficial and vacuous culture. Ironically, it is this emptiness that points toward, according to Rossetti's work, a mark of Spanish cultural identity in the wake of the Franco's death (111). The combination also remits to the tendency for combining high culture (represented here by a very stylized reaching toward the sublime) with low culture (the almost vacuous eroticism and use of a commercial image present in the poem). The fact that it is a woman's gaze upon the image of a man, as stated above, emphasizes the shifting of gender roles in the poem, as Rossetti's female poetic subject becomes the active participant in the exchange. It has been recognized that "the seductiveness of the bodies in Rossetti's poetry derives from their conformity to cultural models of eroticism, even when their gender or sexual orientation departs from the norm of these models" (Kruger-Robbins 171). The male image then serves as a cultural icon for her erotic deconstruction of his authority as both male and iconic.

In terms of the Paradigm Shift theory, as stated above Rossetti's work embodies what would seemingly be the adoption of the new, Postmodern paradigm. Yet, by analyzing further the poem's imagery we may observe a less clear-cut process occurring. Although "Chico Wrangler" does not reflect the reconciliation of the traditional with the deconstructive, it does base itself on the motif of the lover's gaze present in late 16th and early 17th Century poetry in Spanish. This fits well, particularly, with

Rossetti's previously noted articulation of past imagery [from the work of Góngora, for example (Ferradáns 27)]. Also, the absence of attempts at defining specifically the state of Spanish society also sets her apart from her contemporaries (Moreiras Menor 115) and binds her work with the case of Ángel González's poetry from the 1970s on. Here we see a trend toward a certain timelessness in her poetry that we may liken to González's poetry of the period. As Rossetti states, " . . . cuando escribes, no existe una sucesión lógica del tiempo. Todo lo que tienes y todo lo que esperas está ahí" (Rossetti 14) (Eng., . . . when you write, the logical passing of time does not exist. All you have and all you hope for is there"). In more general terms (and beyond the scope of the poem cited above), the theme of death, although present in her prose (Moreira Menor 119), does not take a central role in her poetry. I believe that this is due to Rossetti's adherence to the experiencing of a postmodern ideal which, in its ambiguous, indefinable and nihilistic view of the decentralized universe, sees the attempt to transcend the world as a waste of time. Death's absence may also reflect the lack of ontological historicity which, in Rossetti's postmodernism, signifies that the meaning of death becomes relative to others' interpretation of it in the present. This reduces its absolute nature to a relativized, and thus less transcendent, poetic and ontological element of both the poetic subject's experience and that subject's view of the external forces which have driven it (and on which I have commented here). Death, as a part of transcendence in both Hierro's and González's work, as well as an important theme traditionally in Spanish poetry, may also reflect the historical aspect of life, one which, in Rossetti's postmodernism, no longer has any meaning (119).

Belén Gopegui is, admittedly, a possibly questionable choice to include in this analysis. This statement comes not as an evaluation of her work, but rather, because Gopegui not known for her poetry—she is a recognized Spanish novelist. I have chosen to include her work in this study due to the nature of her more condensed use of the Spanish language. Particularly in the case of her first novel, *La escala de los mapas* (1993), her more lyrical use of language within the narrative structure has been described as more "a poetic prose (Legido-Quigley 103)" than a more straight-forward narration, such as that found in her contemporaries. The novel itself defines the first phase of Gopegui's writing, that of "philosophical and abstract deliberations (103)" of her characters' psychological processes. Her writing is both socially-aware and intimate, giving the reader of vision of both the interior of the character's psyche as well as the contextualization of that character within 1990s Spain.

This re-imagining of the poetic subject as protagonist of a synchronically based testimonial poetic fits with the sort of de-politicizing of poetry (as a response to changes in social structures from the dictatorial period, as seen above) which occurred in the 90s. In any case, the following excerpt from *La escala de los mapas*, in which the protagonist, Prim, describes a morning in bed with his girlfriend, Brezo, gives us a good idea of how her poetic prose achieves this:

> Por la mañana pobló mi habitación un eco de campanas de río. Daban las nueve, un frío de nubes grises se transparentaba por el cristal. Yo lo veía sin sentirlo. Desde los pies, todo a lo largo de mi costado y hasta el embozo reinaba la hospitalaria temperatura. Con cada movimiento de los párpados me invadía una oleada de placer durmiente, ese intenso alivio que da la sed calmada se repetía, de a poco, en las sucesivas articulaciones. Brezo, el hueco debe de ser un estado semejante a cuando nos movemos bajo las mantas, y afuera hace frío pero en el interior de la cama, como el aire, se agita y nos roza una temperatura que es la justa, la que la sangre quiso y propició en sueños. (Gopegui 125)

> (Eng., "In the morning an eco of river bells populated my room. It was around nine, a cold from gray clouds was made transparent by the glass. I saw it without feeling it. From my feet, along my back and up to the nape a hospitable temperature reigned. With each movement of my eyelids a wave of sleeping pleasure invaded, that intense relief that makes for calm thirst would repeat, little by little, in successive articulations. Brezo, the space should be a similar state to when we move under the blankets, and outside it is cold but in the inside of the bed, like the air, a temperature that is just right comes to life and rubs against us, one that blood wanted and that propagated in dreams." (Translation by Robert Simon)

The image of the cold air in contrast to the heat of the lovers in bed, along with the direct relationship between blood and heat, is an obvious and bordering on kitsch in the context of this intimate scene. There exist a certain consciousness about the external world that becomes internalized through Prim's meditations, as we find in the poetry of both Rossetti when gazing upon the "chico" as well as in previous poetries whose social context is evident, such as that of González. However, the movement of the protagonist's thoughts from the external to the internal experience, from the cold air and foggy windows toward the dream world which the heat of the lovers' bodies creates, takes us to that ultra-intimate universe found in the testimonial poems of Hierro or even to the experimentalist works of Herberto Helder. In fact, the sensations taken from the world outside of Prim's body become so incorporated into his own perspective that even the mention of Brezo's name does nothing more than instigate the next thought, a "hueco," or empty space, which rejects his thoughts about himself and fills instead with thoughts of her (although not with her body, assumingly present with him in the bed). In terms of a postmodern poetic text, the presence of cliché imagery with such a deeper process creates a space for "kitsch," the space being that left between Brezo and Prim, may indicate a derridean "différence" is present and being used to substitute what should be the central space for love and for the lovers' union, another classic yet ironically absent finality in the text.

In terms of placing this text within the greater Paradigm Shift, it seems clear that Gopegui's work fits into what we have defined as the Postmodern paradigm. Its direct application of Derridean space within an intimate, yet deconstructive, context lends to this conclusion. In combination with Rossetti's poetry, the two trajectories define for us two of the primary variants of the postmodern in Spanish poetics in the 1990s: the synchronic strain (that of Gopegui, as seen above) and the diachronic, historical deconstruction of a masculine-based social hegemony.

At this point in the story, then, we are left with what seems to be an adoption of the Postmodern paradigm, albeit with variations that do not look to be in competition with one-another, but mutually exclusive and, thus, functional within the same space. The next step, beyond the Adoption Phase, would then be to see how quickly this Postmodern paradigm begins to break down, as its very nature appears to lend itself to immediate fragmentation. However, this scenario is not likely. As we will see in the somewhat more detailed textual analysis of which the next chapter is composed, as poetic writing becomes more "postmodern," its ability to adapt to other genres, such as that of the various mystical traditions that have existed (and continue to exist) in the peninsula, the Postmodern paradigm as we have conceived of it until now does not entirely cover all literary (and, thus, cultural) possibilities. What should in its conception deconstruct the essentialist discourse of the mystical, then, concedes to combine with it, creating a poetry which, like Peninsular cultures themselves, may not necessarily give way to postmodernism / Postmodernity in their Northern European / North American forms (such as those seen in our discussion of Culler and Hutchison).

# Chapter V: 1975-2000, Clara Janés and Joaquim Pessoa

We have seen in the previous chapters that there exists a possible link between the social, political and artistic evolutions of Spanish and Portuguese societies during the period of 1950 to the 1990s. Poetry, then, has served to reflect abstractly, through the use of new forms, themes and techniques, this evolution. We have also applied Kuhn's theory of the Paradigm Shift to the period, noting the entrance of the Modern paradigm into its Crisis Phase, and then the passing into the Transitional Phase from whence a new, dominant paradigm (supposedly, the Postmodern paradigm) would take hold. The poetic works of Moura in Portugal and Rossetti in Spain have revealed this process to be active. However, in this chapter we will see another current, one whose seemingly contradictory nature will make evident that the process of paradigm adoption is not, in the Iberian context, quite so simple.

Before studying one of the more enigmatic poetic trends that characterizes the Transitional Phase in the Iberian cultures, it may be a good idea to review the historical process leading up to this point. In the 1990s, Spain and Portugal are both active members of the European Union, and are open supporters of the adoption of the Euro as the continent's new currency. Yet, as Spain's development into what neighboring countries would consider civilization, other traditions such as bullfighting are "more popular and fashionable since . . . the sixties (Hooper 357)." It has been noted that even the traditional location of the country's capital, Madrid, reveals a taste for tradition that counteracts the modernizing effect seen in other cities such as Barcelona, "a more progressive city (Crow 434)." The situation in Portugal is also as much a tug-of-war, although that battle may be found better represented in the nation's literary development than in its more subtle social structures. The "revivalism" we spoke of in a previous chapter remits to the fact that "o conceito do Pós-modernismo padece ainda de uma grande indefinição

(Guimarães, *A Poesia Contemporânea*, 172)," (Eng., "the concept of postmodernism suffers still from a great lack of definition"), describing what may seem an "anything goes" attitude taking hold in Portuguese literature. This allows for opposing and often contradictory tendencies (observed both in the Portuguese poetics of which Guimarães speaks, as well as in the classical yet explicitly and strongly deconstructive nature of the work of Spanish poets such as Ana Rossetti). This is not invisible in the social nor in the political strata, however, as despite the country's quick progress in terms of education and democratic reform, "the most difficult challenge . . . remained agricultural reform (Birmingham 192-3)." Through the works of Clara Janés and Joaquim Pessoa, we may see that Spanish and Portuguese poetic lines begin to merge in the late Twentieth Century, although to the detriment of an easy adoption of the Postmodern paradigm.[11]

The trajectory of criticism on Clara Janés has, in the last ten years, taken us from the Erotic used to re-define feminism, to the universal, and finally into the realm of the mystical. The most clearly studied themes in Clara Janés' poetry are centered around an entirely erotic and feminist, anti-hegemonic poet, searching for the origin of essence in the "chora," or pre-linguistic womb, of Kristevan critical thought. As we delve deeper into Janés' apparent deconstruction of the phallic patrimony with her intertextually mystical journey, we find in the cross-over a series of dichotomies, or "binary oppositions," that engender an ambiguous space for the creation and nurturing of a new feminine self. This works because the dichotomous forces brought together in Janés' poetry (the particular vs. the universal) create in their union an ambiguous (and thus, free) highly erotic space. Within this space, the exclusion of the (male) lover's active participation in the more profound aspects of the erotic experience gives rise to a new, uniquely free and universal feminine identity.

Janés' poetry from the beginning of her career reflects a deep interest in a search for that which is the most essential, while at the same time attempting to transcend national, physical psychological and literary limits (Wilcox, *Clara Janés*, 356). Her constant investigation of the internalized self differentiates her from what Wilcox characterizes as a more masculine, extroverted voice (357). In the poem "Rosa del desierto" (*Vivir* 15), for example, the poetic voice describes the scent of the rose (a

---

11. I should note that, though the summaries of both poets' works to follow may be found in various forms in my previous scholarship, I do intend to recontextualize both Janes' and Pessoa's work within that of the Paradigm Shift theory.

symbol of fecundity and the female genitalia) as it transforms into the witness (and thus carrier) of its own plenitude:

> Las rosas rojas de indetenible aliento
> cuya energía núbil de capullo
> en esplendor y aroma se transforma,
> testigo son de plenitud y de tránsito.
> Esta pequeña piedra, sin embargo,
> no entra en competencia con el tiempo,
> no le teme al no ser, pues ser le basta,
> y bellamente, en silencio total,
> la perfección de lo imposible muestra.

> (Eng. "The red roses and unstoppable breath
> whose nubile energy from a bud
> is transformed in splendor and aroma,
> witness they are of plenitude and transition.
> This small stone, nonetheless,
> does not complete with time,
> is not afraid of not being, since being is enough,
> and beautifully, in total silence,
> the perfection of the impossible it shows")
> (Translation by Robert Simon)

The absence of any sort of symbol or metaphor referring to the opposite sex is important as it allows for the exploration of this feminine symbol for its own sake. It does not depend on any phallic referent to define itself. Also, by focusing on the invisible, floating scent of the rose rather than on its physical form, the poetic voice allows the rose to transcend its physical limitations and to become "la perfección de lo imposible." Temporality becomes a moot point for the poetic voice, as the scent of the rose transcends the perceived limits of death.[12] Thus, a profound and perpetual questioning of Western, masculinized values comes into effect in Janés' poetry, which deconstructs, then rewrites, some of our conceptions of the notion of Women. Thus far, then, Janés' poetry seems to differ little from the purpose of Rossetti's, that is, it deconstructs metaphorically the masculine hegemony present in Spanish culture. As we continue our analysis, however, we will observe that the difference in method will differentiate of Janés' (and Pessoa's) poetry within the context of the apparent and proven paradigm shift.

---

12. It should be noted that the juxtaposition of love/sex and death is a traditional combination in Spanish poetry throughout its history. It is found in the works of twentieth-century poets such as Lorca, Alexandre, Alberti and many others.

The weakening of the masculine in Janés' poetic voice and the deconstruction of that masculinity need a space, however, in which to occur. In fact, in "Rosa del desierto," cited above, as well as throughout *Vivir*, the poetic ego simply does not appear. On the rare occasion that it does, such as in "Gato" or "Una Paloma," the poetic ego appears in reference only to an element of nature to be poeticized (in these cases, the animals who make up the title of each poem), and not for its own sake. Thus, a uniquely feminine identity emerges in the union of feminine sexuality and poetic creativity, expressed through the presence of erotic corporeal pleasures combined with music, a pre-linguistic state of reflection (Keefe Ugalde 312). This relationship extends itself, beginning with *Kampa*, into the realm of nature, as the unrestricted nature, or fluidity, of the poetic self (which Keefe Ugalde designates as feminine) come to form an integral part of the poetic ego (313). Thus, we see the emergence of a unbound feminine poetic self whose true meaning lies not within the confines of the male (and thus phallic) lover, but within her own singular, intimate and eroticized relationship with the exterior world.

We may explain this phenomenon as the process whereby the deconstruction of the masculine becomes fecund (able to create life) in the context of a non-masculine erotic (and here, poetic) experience. Along with, and as a direct consequence of, this erotic deconstruction of sexuality as a fixed, gender-based value, we find ourselves in a poetic world with neither physical nor hierarchical limits. "Talvez la manifestaciones más importantes de la identidad femenina en la poesía de Clara . . . son la preponderancia de la unión y la fluidez y la ausencia de un orden jerárquico (Keefe Ugalde 312)." (Eng., "Perhaps the most important manifestations of feminine identity in Clara's poetry . . . are the preponderance of union and the fluidity and absence of a hierarchic order"). As a consequence, the universal femininity of the chora gives rise to what we may classify as the *feminine* act of literary creation. Again, the shift into the Postmodern paradigm seems so far complete and uncomplicated. Once more, however, the purpose of this study is not to reveal the simplicity of the process; rather, in this case it will make evident the contradictory complexity of the process of the paradigm shift in the contemporary Iberian context.

In Ugalde's article, *Huellas de la mujer en la poesía de Clara Janés*, we begin to see the first real in-depth analysis of Janés's search the kristevan "chora," or origin of life and creation, in her poetry (Keefe Ugalde, *Huellas*, 203). Ugalde summarizes the "chora" as a term coined by the postmodern feminist theorist Julia Kristeva, who re-named the notion of the uterine space using the Greek term for the uterus, or "chora." According to Ugalde, Kristeva identifies this space with the semiotic in terms of its function as a "pre-oedipal" (and thus, non-masculine and non-erotic, in Freudian psychological theory), disorganized combination of sound, movement and the basic impulses of our animal beginnings (202). The semiotic, is seems, subverts the notion of organized language as an ideal, revealing it as having stemmed from a phallocentric concept of society (202). Thus, the notion of the "chora," as it appears in Janés' poetry, serves to deconstruct this (assumedly) masculine ideal by purposefully disorganizing it, breaking it down into its most basic (i.e., essential) and animal-like structures to demonstrate its hypocritical nature as both an ideal means of communication and a method for the suppression of the feminine.

This search for the chora, or uterine space, appears in such works as *Kampa II* and *Vivir*. According to Ugalde, Janés, in these works, articulates not only a break-down of the "normal" rhythms of language as an attack on the masculine symbolic, but recorded tapes to emphasize in her poetry that which is "un fluir prelingüístico desorganizado" (Eng., "a disorganized, pre-linguistic flow") of sound, and rhythm (202-3). The final section of *Vivir*, "Planto," is composed entirely of verse put to musical notation, an approximation to the "pre-linguistic fluidity" noted above (*Vivir* 65-76). The fact that we find poetry in both Spanish and Catalan indicates the unimportance of a particular language, highlighting then the importance of sound and musicality over semantic meaning. The song "Ah!" (69), for example, is made up of a C-major progression and the syllable "a" triumphantly exclaimed. This short melody, thus, is based on the sound made with the mouth entirely open, as an animal or baby's cry. It is also a sound made as death takes the body, as in the song before it whose final verses are "presente / el cuerpo / de muerte" (68) (Eng., "present / the body / of death"). The musical score that accompanies is not at all intricate. Rather, it is a simple tune from which it is possible to create many other possible melodies. So, here we have a space for possible future creation based on that which is most basic and essential—the musical "chora," as it were, borne from the union of creation and death, another dichotomous relationship.

Despite our critical assertions of Janés as a feminist, anti-phallic and chora-seeking poet, as early as 1988, in an interview with Keefe Ugalde, she makes statements which should lead us to question our interpretation of her work as purely postmodern. In this interview, Janés clarifies that she sees herself as taking part in a (highly mystical) poetic tradition beginning with San Juan de la Cruz (Keefe Ugalde, *Conversaciones*, 45). Janés also makes references in the interview to Sappho, Murasaki ("una japonesa que vivió entre el siglo X y el XI"), Sor Juana Inés de la Cruz, among many other poets (45-47), as points of personal artistic inspiration. Later, she goes on to comment that she doesn't feel she pertains to a decidedly feminist literature (46). If, after all of the argumentation presented on Janés as a feminist writer, she still does not see herself as such, what then does that say about the validity of our more feminist analysis? More importantly, what function does she see herself fulfilling through her poetry, if not the one designated here? At one point in the interview, Janés affirms that her poetry is a "constante búsqueda de la luz." She also states that the experience of the exterior world is an "experiencia visionaria, una «visión», lo que . . . podríamos decir, es la identificación con lo «otro» . . . creo que está muy vinculado a la cuestión de la luz (49)." These clear affirmations of a mystical nature do not necessarily contradict the anti-phallic, anti-hegemonic development of the chora as Kristeva has conceived of it. They do, however, force us to revise our critical stance and take into account a kind of mystical journey which Janés, upon contemplation of her own suicide, has undertaken. At the end of the interview, Keefe Ugalde asks Janés, "¿ha sido la poesía una salvación, incluso del suicidio?" (Eng., "Has poetry been a salvation, particularly from suicide?") Her answer is the following, "Sí, lo ha sido . . . porque a mí me había salvado de la muerte, me había hecho seguir viviendo (50)." (Eng., "Yes, it has . . . because it had saved me from death, had made me keep on living."). Thus, despite her arguable adherence to a feminist ideology, the purpose of her poetry, due especially to its mystical nature, is not only one of female empowerment, but of personal enlightenment, salvation, and the re-invention of her historical Iberian identity. It is precisely this mystical vein that will distinguish both Janés and Pessoa as counter to the "pure" Postmodern paradigm, complicating the matter of paradigm adoption as one whose seeming evidence may suddenly be questioned.

We should now turn our attention, given the elucidation offered in the above-referenced interview, to the presence of mysticism as a singular influence and all-encompassing theme in Janés' poetry. We should keep in mind that, while informative, the studies by Engelsen Marson, Keefe Ugalde and Francis do not clearly define this mysticism any more that Janés herself does in her interview.

Ellen Engelsen Marson, in 1995, published her article *Clara Janés: Mysticism and the Search for the Female Poetic Voice*. In this work we see that, for the first time, the topic of mysticism is studied as an independently fluid (i.e., unrestricted and defining) concept in Janés' poetry. Engelsen Marson divides this Janesian mystical process into three stages, "purgation," "illumination" and "union with the Absolute," coinciding with the stages of the mystical journey as described by Santa Teresa (245), San Juan de la Cruz's mentor. The first stage is that of purification through pain, where the soul of the sufferer becomes empty, ready thus to be filled by "binary oppositions," such as "love" and "pain." The actual receiving of the binary oppositions constitutes the second stage. This then prepares the mystic's soul for the third stage, its union with God (245).

In *Vivir* we find the poem "Teoría" opening the collection (9):

Contra dolor amor se intensifica,
dota de tacto al pensamiento en el objeto,
toma cuerpo en las voces que el mármol no retiene,
en las epifanías de gélida materia;
arremete en turbiones contra sombra,
da vuelo al pie que discurre entre las yerbas,
y desata del tiempo aquí mutante
la pura transparencia.

(Eng., "Against pain love is intensified,
it dotes touch onto thought in the object,
it takes a body in the voices that marble does not retain,
in the epiphanies of gelid matter;
it attacks shadow in squalls,
it gives flight to the foot that scurries among the grasses,
and unties from the here mutable time
pure transparency.")
(Translation by Robert Simon)

We are able to conclude that there exists in this poem a mystical process whereby pain and love drive toward transcendence. Ontologically speaking, the poetic voice introduces a contrast of the material versus the sublime and in so doing intertwines the mystical with the ontological. Then, through the absence of a strong poetic ego in the poem, the theme of transcendence becomes a universal one.

Still, the definition of the term "mysticism" cannot be wholly drawn from Renaissance Christian sources. As seen above, the mystical process coincides ontologically and semiotically with the quest for the chora, a postmodern deconstruction of the phallocentric *par excellence*. In fact, Natalia Francis' dissertation, completed in 1998, includes a chapter dedicated to Janés' expression of mysticism, either through the characters, places or themes portrayed in her work, combined with her postmodern tendencies. Thus, we see that Janés produces a very uniquely ambiguous mystical deconstruction based in, as we have noted, the simultaneity and union of opposing dualities. Francis is also the first to mention Sufism, although in a relatively limited scope, in any critical work written on Janés. According to Francis, whose conclusions differ from those of Keefe Ugalde, Janés does not so much revise myth as she does recreate and, thus, renew myth within her own contemporary poetic context (153). Francis also states first that myth in Janés' work carries an ontological meaning (154), a notion which, as we have seen in the poem "Teoría," makes logical sense. It stands to reason, then, that her preoccupation with the deconstruction of the masculine-dominated Western discourse finds itself deeply entrenched in the fight against those primordial elements of our phallocentrist mythology.

However, the deconstruction of myth and mysticism isn't so important in and of itself. Rather, we should view this process as a reconstruction under a more pro-feminine discourse. This idea coincides with my own exploration of Janés' work as a re-centralization of the erotic as fluid, and thus feminine, within the space created by the deconstructed ontological and semiotic state. In the poem "Soy la abeja" from *Creciente Fértil* (24), we see the physical nature of the female poetic voice as one of a sexual body and as one of a bee come to pollinate the male (an obvious inversion):

> Soy la abeja enviada en pos de ti, ¡oh Telipinu!
> En ebrio vuelo emprenderé el acoso;
> tomaré cera y lavaré tu cuerpo
> melado como el ámbar;
> te picaré en las manos y en los pies,
> despertaré insolente tu capullo
> y podré al fin libar.
> Y de una gota desataré una fuente
> con labios deslizantes,
> cubriéndote a batidas
> hasta enjutar tu orto,
> para que te sometas
> exangüe a mi dominio.

> (Eng., "I am the bee sent to you, Oh Telipinu!
> In drunken flight I will undertake the pursuit;
> I will take wax and wash your body
> tanned like ambar;
> I will peck your hands and your feet,
> I will awaken your bud insolently

and will be able finally to imbibe.
And from a drop I will undo a fountain
with slippery lips,
covering you with whipping
until I fill your star's rising,
so that you submit
purified to my dominion.")
          (Translation by Robert Simon)

The pro-feminine discourse, as throughout *Creciente Fértil*, comes from the aftermath of the deconstructed state of the male discourse. The bee, once a symbol of male fecundity and fluidity, now becomes appropriated by the female poetic voice. Telipinu, who Janés explains at the beginning of the collection is the mythical son of the Goddess Auriga (11), is reduced to the simple recipient of her advances. As for any mystical yearnings in the poem, the combination of love and pain (the poetic voice's stinging him) as the path to purification (as "exangüe" to her dominion) resonate from our definition of mysticism into three stages, as seen earlier.

However, probably the most detailed analysis of the mystical in Janés' poetry comes from that of Candelas Newton. Here we see an analysis of the manifestation of myth and mysticism as an attack on the patriarchal and phallocentric hegemony through the presence of non-Christian (and, thus, non-phallic) themes (110). This would make any "non-Christian" discourse a move against that language (at least for the sake of Newton's argument). In any case, we may easily confirm this mythical intertextuality in our analysis of "Soy la abeja" above. We then emerge with yet another duality based on the utilization of the contemporary, namely, the search for the feminine self as a universal and as the negation of masculine power as represented in a more traditional mystical quest. The presence of the Goddess Inanna through whom the poetic voice in *Creciente Fértil* begins its quest for divine illumination, the notions of transubstantiation, and the use of magic combine to defy traditional Christian thought, according to Dr. Newton (111). It should be noted, nonetheless, that the mysticism analyzed so far has been seen as a Christian one, meaning essentially that *not all* Christian thought is simply negated in Janés' work. "Soy la abeja," with its mystical purification, is a perfect example of this. Besides that, the supposed dichotomy of elements of Christian Neo-Platonic *mysticism* and Pre-Judaic Middle-Eastern *mythology* do not actually exist in binary opposition to one another. This means that they are not able to support the type of contrast in opposition needed so that Janés' poetry may produce the effects discussed above. This effect may be found more explicitly in Janes' later works, such as *Diván y el ópalo de fuego* (1996). The importance of Janés' poetry to the study of the paradigm shift is that her work develops a functional duality between the mystical and the postmodern with both deconstructs the male hegemonic structures and preserves an essentialist vision which, in principle, the Postmodern paradigm should not allow.

The case of Joaquim Pessoa differs from that of Clara Janés, at first glance, both thematically and critically.[13] Thematically, his focus seems more on social issues, such as censorship (as I will discuss in detail throughout this section), while Janés' does not. Critically, we find comments on his work in the critical writings of Saraiva, Guimarães and in several relatively unknown critical works, yet nothing more than that. At times we even find critical interpretations made not from any poetic analysis, but from what Pessoa himself may say (without any substantiation through critical analysis) about his own poetry. Such is the case of his supposed realism inherited from Cesário Verde. The name appears at the end of the poem "As palavras do meu canto" as the invocation of another poet who loves his city (Lisbon) and his country (Pessoa, *Vol I*, 99). Saraiva seems to take this as something more than simply a coincidental similarity or minor formal influence (*História*, 1125), despite relatively little proof in Pessoa's actual poetry to support this belief.[14]

In any case, we may divide Pessoa's work, both diachronically and thematically, into three stages. The first is the stage of deconstruction; the second is that of a metaphoric, mystical exploration into the tragic, ontological irony surrounding the themes borne from the first; the third, and most recent, is the stage which I refer to as that of the search for a representation of the self. Thematically speaking, we may observe Joaquim's adherence in the 1970s to the technique of deconstruction as a tool against the use of poetry as a function of state legitimacy, and poetry's subsequent reconstruction as a tool for the protection of poetic freedom in the context of a society betrayed by its own anti-totalitarian social revolution. I will then continue with an analysis of themes such as the freedom of the poetic word, and the silencing / self-censoring of that word. There is an evident presence of a mystical journey in Pessoa's

---

13. Please refer to *Understanding the Portuguese Poet Joaquim Pessoa, 1942-2007: A Study in Iberian Cultural Hybridity* (the Edwin Mellen Press, 2008) for a more detailed study of Joaquim Pessoa's work.
14. Please refer to *Understanding the Poet Joaquim Pessoa: 1942-2007 . . .* for more information on this issue.

more metaphysically-inclined poetry which, from the 1980s to the beginning of the 21st Century, takes center stage.

Pessoa's poetic evolution, while complex, also is indicative of the apparent adoption, yet simultaneous challenging, of the Postmodern paradigm as defined here, as visible even in his own poetry and in sectors of the society at large. We must remember that the context, one of struggle between the traditionalist and "modernized" society is one that has not ended in Portuguese (nor in Spanish) society and political decision-making. So, while reading the analysis below we must remain conscientious of this division and the relationship between the mystical, yet deconstructive, tendencies in this poetry, as well as in Janés'.

The process of deconstruction is evident in one of Pessoa's first works, *Apenas Caminhar* (1972), which as incorporated later into *O Pássaro no Espelho* (1975). In the poem "Livre e Vertical," for example, we may observe deconstruction acting upon a symbolism present in Portuguese poetry of the 1960's and 70's:

> O pé fincado na espuma branca
> na leve areia poalha destes astros
> que respiram o dia pelos troncos, árvores.
> Pelas pedras já voam devagar
> os exactos pássaros devorando
> outros grãos de sol e trigo, areia.
>
> Já sabemos de cor estas manhãs
> Tão altas e apenas meio-dia
> e já os passos ressoam cavos altos
> pela sombra dos corpos e dos olhos.
> Não há por entre as ruas outras ruas.
>
> Escrevo os versos com sangue disponível
> dos pássaros que arremesso contra o espelho.
> Caminho livre e vertical dobrando
> o finíssimo equilíbrio das manhãs.
>     (35)
>
> (Eng., "the foot sunk into the white foam
> the light sand dusts from these stars
> that breath the day through their trunks, trees.
> Through the stones they slowly fly
> the exact birds devouring
> other grains of sun and wheat, sand.
>
> We already know these mornings by heart
> so tall and just mid-day
> and already the steps sound out high concave arches

through the shadow of bodies and eyes.
There are no streets between the other streets.

I write verses with available blood
of the birds that I hurl against the mirror.
I walk free and vertical doubling
the exquisite balance of mornings.")
        (Translation by Robert Simon)

The first stanza of the poem contains an enumeration of symbols from nature which I have proven in previous scholarship to be related to the Sufi mystical process, a system which will become more explicit later on in Pessoa's work. In any case, the poetic subject views this world by looking from his feet in the sand to the birds in the sky, drawing a vertical line in the world which reminds us of the poem's title. Also, the poetic subject's feet are planted firmly in the sand, connecting him with a world which the birds devour. This image should remind us of the image of the bird as the poetic word from Herberto Helder's "O Amor em Visita" (Helder 30), as well as the poetic subject's submission to the will and the force of nature in both "Amor em Visita" and Ruy Belo's "Homem Perto do Chão" (Belo, *Obra*, 20). Thus, we have established the first point of the deconstructive text, that of a text which works within the boundaries set by the deconstructed object, in this case the symbolism establish by the Helder and the poets of "Poesia 61" and of related poets such as Ruy Belo. This evident break from the poets who had brought forth the type of experimentalist and intimate poetics so necessary for postmodernism (and whose poetry we have analyzed and contextualized in previous chapters) takes on a dual meaning. The first is Pessoa's desire to return to a socially-based poetry, similar in scope to that of Moura although becoming more mystically inclined in the 1980s. The second, that of the need to find the solid base which the postmodern poetic will then deconstruct some recognizable, cultural artifice (in this case, the hierarchy of man to nature), fits cleanly with the analysis thus far.

The second stanza expresses the first questioning of the system, in which the poetic subject submits itself to nature. Here, the poetic subject states the repetitiveness of the symbols used in the first stanza, describing them as steps that "sound out high concave arches / through the shadow of bodies and eyes." They neither contain, nor have the capacity to become, any more than the empty shell of what once had meaning. In terms of deconstruction, this statement renders moot the power of the signifiers from the first stanza, as, due to overuse / abuse in previous poetry and by previous poets, they no longer carry any semantic weight. The final statement of the poem, "There are no streets between the other streets" is an interestingly ambiguous phrase semantically, as the designation of the original streets as "other" inverts the hierarchical structure set up in both the beginning of the stanza as well as the beginning of the poem. Thus, Pessoa has not just questioned the semiotic of an established symbolic hierarchy; he has also deconstructed and inverted, or reversed, the logic behind the causality through which the deconstructed object created its own notion of the power of its poetic word.

The last stanza is, as far as I am concerned, the most original and important of the poem. Here, rather than leaving the deconstructed object in its embarrassingly uncovered, fragmented state, Pessoa's poetic subject re-writes the poetic process so that the signifier may again reflect the existence of the signified. This move, although not necessarily contrary to the purpose of deconstruction, does allow for the future inclusion of various other methods of "reconstruction" of poetry and of the manner by which the signifier's meaning is returned to it. One of these methods, the Sufi Mystical process as re-written by Pessoa, will become that much more important later on.

In any case, in the final stanza we see that the mirror is the tool by which one may see himself in his most superficial representation, without the depth of the spirit or personality expressed. The bird, or poetic word, must be deconstructed by exposing it to its own superficiality in order that it may be freed from the abuse suffered from what Pessoa evidently views as previous poets' fallacious idealism. The final verses of the poem, "walking freely and vertically doubling / the exquisite balance of mornings," is a statement of empowerment in which the poetic subject's deconstruction of the poetic word allows him to move freely both in the world of nature (the horizontal axis of the poem) and the sublime world of imagination in which the poetic word travels (the vertical axis of the poem, not accessible to the poetic subject in the first stanza). The self-affirmation as a free poetic subject, thus, happens only through the process of deconstruction.

So, it seems that Pessoa has taken steps similar to those of Moura, with an even more critical deconstructive focus. As in the case of Janés, we see what appears to be the adoption of a Postmodern paradigm as reflected in a poetic medium. As the 1980s progress we see the thematic focus turning inward, then searching for a mystical answer to the problem of love and its unrequited nature. Finally, in the 1990s (as we will see in the example below), the two tendencies join in a manner that both links Pessoa's poetry to that of Janés, and divides the two in terms of their thematic intentions.

The final section of *Vou-me Embora de Mim* (65-66), one of Pessoa's later works, speaks of a battle where the reader's manner of "suffering" in the world is in conflict with his true nature. The poetic subject tries to explain this through deconstructing the reader's "suffering" and then providing the reader with a way out:

Um anjo diz que sim o outro diz que não.
O poeta diz talvez. E tu que dizes? Tu que vives
a vida de fora para dentro, comandado
por estímulos que entram maquilhados no teu sono e no teu sonho
e que acordam contigo sem alguma vez te terem despertado.      5
Sofres porque habitas um palácio imaginário.
Sofres porque sabes como te chamas mas ignoras quem és.
Sofres porque fechas as janelas da tua casa e as janelas do teu espírito
mas a vida não pára de preparar surpresas
para quando abrires a porta na manhã seguinte.      10
Sofres porque cada orgasmo é uma festa maravilhosa que te estremece apenas o
[corpo.
Sofres porque cada satisfação tua foi atingida com um imenso rol de profundas
insatisfações
Sofres porque quase sempre o que tu desejas não é o que tu queres.
Sofres porque não vais além do coração e porque o coração
não vai além de ti. E porque ambos se atrapalham.      15
Sofres porque tens medo e porque tens medo de ter medo.
Sofres porque tens dificuldade em olhar para a frente, partir de ti para um outro
[tu,
e porque olhar fixamente para trás te pode transformar numa estátua de sal.
Sofres porque a tua honestidade é desonesta e a tua consciência é um juiz
que tu mesmo te encarregas de corromper. Sofres      20
porque a tua infâmia pode preencher a primeira página
e porque a primeira página nunca fala de ti nem que seja para mostrar a tua
[infâmia.
Sofres porque é grande a sensação de ameaça
e porque enorme é o tédio e porque é fundo o desespero.
Sofres porque as razões porque és feliz são as mesmas razões da tua
[infelicidade.      25
Sofres porque sabes tudo isto e desconheces tudo isto
e porque o conhecimento das coisas e o desconhecimento das coisas
são sempre a primeira e a última das razões
para invocares o teu inútil sofrimento.


(Eng., "One angel says yes and another one says no.
The poet says maybe. And what do you say? You who lives
life outside to in, commanded
by stimulus that enter all made up in your sleep and in your dreams
and that awaken with you without ever having awakened you.      5

You suffer because you live in an imaginary palace.
You suffer because you know your name but you ignore who you are.
You suffer because you close the windows of your house and the windows of
your spirit
but life doesn't stop making surprises
for when you open the door the next day.                    10
You suffer because every orgasm is an awesome party that makes only your
body shudder.
You suffer because every satisfaction of yours was reached with an important
role of profound dissatisfactions
You suffer because what you desire is almost never what you want.
You suffer because you don't go further than the heart and because the heart
doesn't go further than you. And because you both hinder
[each other.                                                 15
You suffer because you're afraid and because you're afraid of being afraid.
You suffer because you find looking forward difficult, leaving yourself for [an-
other you,
and because looking fixedly behind you can turn you into a pillar of salt.
You suffer because your honesty is dishonest and your conscience is a judge
that you yourself are dedicated to corrupting. You suffer          20
because your infamy can fill up the first page
and because the first page never speaks of you even if to show your infamy.
You suffer because the threatened feeling is great
And because your boredom is enormous and your desperation deep.
You suffer because the reasons you're happy are the same for your
[unhappiness.                                                25
You suffer because you know all of this and don't know any of it
and because your knowledge of things and your ignorance of things
are always the first and the final reasons
for you to invoke your useless suffering.")
      (Translation by Robert Simon)

The fragment begins with the recognition of an internal conflict, that of the opposing voices which exist in every person. These voices form a binary opposition which serves the basis for our capacity for judgment and logical thought. The second verse refers to the notion of the poet as a third voice, remitting back to the notion that the truth is a three-edged sword, one being person A's perception, another person B's, and the last being the truth. The reference to the poet as "perhaps saying it," then, designates the poet as being the closest to the truth. The notion also reminds the reader of the authoritative stand that poets took in the early Twentieth century as the greatest, and sometimes only, perceivers of the truth. (This seemingly retrograde tendency in Pessoa's work, from an extremely postmodern, deconstructionist standpoint to one whose characteristics seem more akin to Modernism's authoritative perspective is, in part, a consequence of the presence and influence of Sufi mystical im-

agery, symbols and notions in Pessoa's second stage.) From the end of
the second verse to the end of the poem Pessoa's poetic subject, having
already passed through the stages of deconstruction, mystical illumina-
tion and purification, and postmodern self-analysis (in the present collec-
tion), deconstructs the interlocutor's "suffering." He states first that the
interlocutor lives his life "from outside to within," as opposed to the
more illuminated method of living which may be inferred from Pessoa's
work, that is, from within to understand that which exists outside of the
mind. The poetic subject continues, saying that the stimulus which enters
from the outside "enters made-up [with make-up] in your sleep and in
your dreams." This reference to the truth made "prettier" through distor-
tion and covering-up reminds us of the references to the truth as a tor-
tured and crazed horse from Pessoa's first stage, as well as to artistic
methods of distortion, such as Valle-Inclán's "esperpento." The "esper-
pento," of course, was a method of twisting the outside, as though
through a concave mirror, to reveal the true ugliness of fin-de-sècle Eu-
ropean civilization. This fact makes the reference to a truth distorted by
the interlocutor's own mind, rather than by an outside force, even more
significant. This carnavalesque "esperpento," then, sets the stage for the
poetic subject to enter into this distortion, twist it again through a tech-
nique of deconstruction, then hand it back to the interlocutor with all of
the illogical and contradictory processes revealed, which the interlocutor
uses to hide himself from the truth of a universe made of binary opposi-
tions that he himself embodies.

The images brought into being throughout the poem are ironic and il-
logical contradictions that show the deconstructive and simultaneously
reconstructive process above. The difference in meaning between the
verbs "acordar" and "despertar," the latter being a spiritual awakening
while the former an awakening from physical sleep, becomes important
in the fifth verse given the deconstructive technique described above. In
the seventh verse, the interlocutor's recognition of his name and simulta-
neous ignorance of who he is represents a binary opposition between the
name given to the physical manifestation of the self versus the person's
"true name." Verse eight revives the image of the open window, present
in "Primeira Canção de Lisboa" as the opened heart of the poetic subject.
Here, the link is made explicitly between the interlocutor's closed win-
dow and his closed heart, both images of a self-censoring from within
and a deliberate ignorance of what lies outside. Yet in the ninth and tenth
verses, the interlocutor cannot escape the "surprises" of the outside
world, as he must face it "the following morning." This idea, in conjunc-

tion with the poetic subject's hurling of binary oppositions at the inter-
locutor, demonstrates the ridiculousness of the latter's attitude toward the
true nature of the world around him. This application of mystical tenden-
cies to a postmodern deconstruction reveals not only the ability to com-
bine the two, but also the necessity, according to this poetic subject, of
the utility of both in a contemporary context. For the Postmodern para-
digm this is problematic as it accepts precisely the same centralizing
force that the paradigm cannot allow.

The idea of sex takes a primary role in the remainder of the poem.
Verses 11-12 speak of the unsatisfying sexual experience of having "only
the body" feeling sexual pleasure [and that after having suffered so many
"dissatisfactions" that the satisfaction of sexual gratification has little
positive effect]. The 13th verse is one of the more telling in terms of the
word-games played by the Pessoan poetic subject who now has a distinc-
tive understanding of, and control over, both language and deconstruc-
tion. This verse translates as "you suffer because almost always what you
desire is not what you want." The subtle difference in meaning of each
verb marks the confusion present in the interlocutor, caused by an igno-
rance of the binary oppositions which exist within him and which at-
tempt constantly to show him the true path (to illumination, as it were).
The desire expressed, thus, is a reaction to the confusion, rather than an
expression of the spirit's need (or "want") of something more profound.
The sexual experience in the previous verses seems to represent the pro-
cess – the interlocutor desires sex, neither because it gives any spiritual
pleasure nor because the spirit wants it, but because it provides a tempo-
rary, limited satisfaction to the physical body. This limitedness can be
seen as a sign of the body's impure nature, a notion studied in my analy-
sis of poetry from Pessoa's second stage. The "desire," then, is a false
want, as without spiritual pleasure it retains no true value. The real de-
sire, of course, is that which stems from the spirit's "want" of something,
a desire that could be seen as limitless, sublime and "pure," in contrast to
that which is "impure," or the male physical body without that of the fe-
male to purify him. The interlocutor may perceive this "want" if he pays
attention to the binary oppositions which make up the essence of the uni-
verse. Because he seems not to believe, however, that there exists any
other mode of living other than the corporeal, and thus impure, existence
of suffering and the confusion caused by ignoring his spiritual side, he is
doomed to a life of having the truth masked from him. Again, the im-
portance of the spiritual over the over-thought logic of the interlocutor
creates a space in which the deconstructive may itself become decon-

structed by a more centralizing force. This irony, although somewhat extreme, also puts to the question the viability of the Postmodern paradigm, a trait of the Transition Phase according to Kuhn's theory.

In this poem the poetic subject also makes evident the interlocutor's egotism as a partial cause for his existential confusion. Here the interlocutor does not achieve a "purer" form of pleasure because, as the reader may infer, the interlocutor is so wrapped up in himself that he does not open the "windows" of his spirit to what the other may offer. He is surprised by the issues that arise through his own ignorance of the world's binary oppositions, as well as his own, because he does not open himself up to the possibility of their existence. Rather, he sees only what the impure body sees: suffering, dissatisfaction, and a lack of understanding that feeds his suffering in a vicious cycle of ignorance. This cycle is reflected in the final four verses of the poem, where the poetic subject states that the interlocutor "knows" and "is unfamiliar with" the binary oppositions, one of which has just been mentioned and resides in the interlocutor's own self-created confused existence. The poetic subject then declares that the interlocutor's "familiarity" and "unfamiliarity" are his "first and last reasons / to invoke [his] useless suffering." Again, the cycle of knowing and ignoring for the sake of a dissatisfaction which feeds his suffering may give the interlocutor's body the chance for periodic pleasures, but it does not aid him in opening himself to the sublime pleasure of the possibility of "purity."

The corporealness of the interlocutor's situation is also emphasized in verses 14-15, when the poetic subject indicates that the interlocutor never goes beyond his "heart," (a Sufi symbol of the lovers' spiritual meeting place and that it never goes beyond him. The interlocutor and his heart seem to be intertwined in such a way as not to allow either to move beyond the other. The heart is trapped with the man, and thus both hinder and confuse themselves and each other (hence the ambiguity in the verb "se atrapalham.") Given the corporeal, egotistical nature of the interlocutor's existence and the confusion brought about through his ignorance of his more "pure" side, this hindrance of the heart's "want" for going beyond the man makes sense. The remaining verses of the poem, verses 16-25, take on the role of giving more examples to support the notions described above.

Again, the Pessoan universe, as it has evolved from the 1970's up to this point, functions on two central ideas. First, that love is the basic nutrient of existence, and second, that existence is constructed from infinite and constantly present binary oppositions. By presenting the binary oppositions inherent in the interlocutor, the poetic subject has revealed that the interlocutor's ignorance of them is the root of his suffering. The implication of this, of course, is the importance of these binary oppositions, as they signify, as stated above, that within him the notion of love and the possibility of a life with greater meaning still exist. Thus, the "way out" that I have alluded to above is that by deconstructing the problem (i.e., the interlocutor's ignorance of his essential nature), the poetic subject has revealed the solution, that is, the simultaneous binary oppositions themselves, nurtured by love, from which the universe is created. In this way, the marginalized heart from the previously analyzed fragment may be freed and the "desert" of the interlocutor's existence may become "fertile."

A later work of Pessoa's, *Nomes* (Eng., *Names*), deals with similar issues, although repeating the mystical context sought in earlier works. The first poem of the collection is titled "Alexandra:"

Há pequenas aves que têm raízes nas palavras,
Essas palavras que não ficam arrumadas com decência na literatura,
palavras de amantes sem amor, gente que sofre
e a quem falta o ar quando faltam as palavras.
Quando digo o teu nome há uma ave que levanta vôo
como se tivesse nascido o dia e uma brisa encarcerada nas amêndoas
se soltasse para a impelir para o mais frio, para o mais alto, para o mais azul.
Quando volto para casa o teu nome vai comigo
e ao mesmo tempo espera-me já numa casa construída com dois nomes
como se tivesse duas frentes, uma para a montanha e outra para o mar.
Por vezes dou-te o meu nome e fico com o teu,
espreito então por janelas de onde se vêem coisas que nunca antes tinha visto,
coisas que adivinhava mas que não sabia,
coisas que sempre soube mas que nunca quis olhar.
Nessas alturas o meu nome é o teu olhar, e os meus olhos
são justamente a pronúncia do teu nome que se diz
com um pequeno brilho molhado, um som pequeno como um roçagar de asas
dessas aves que constroem o ninho na folhagem da fala
e criam raízes fundas nas palavras vulgares
que os vulgares amantes engradecem
quando falam de amor.
     (15)

(Eng., "There are small birds that take root in words,
These words that do not remain arranged with decency in literature,
a lover's words without love, people who suffer
and without breath when the words are absent.
When I say your name there is a bird that lifts off
as if the day had been borne and a breeze imprisoned in the almonds
were freed to drive on to the greatest cold, to the highest, to the most blue.

When I return home your name goes with me
and at the same time it awaits me in a home already built with two names
as if there were two fronts, one to the mountain and one to the sea.
Sometimes I give you my name and keep yours,
I spy on you then through windows from where come things I have never seen,
things I guessed about but did not know,
things I always knew but refused to see.
At those times my name is your gaze, and my eyes
are simply the pronouncing of your name that is said
with a small, wet shine, a little sound like a brushing of wings
of those birds who build their nest in the foliage of speech
and create deep roots in common words
that common lovers make great
when they speak of love.")
        (Translation by Robert Simon)

One of our first points of focus is the image of the birds ("as aves") that appears wandering throughout the poem's rich imagery. This image, as seen in previous scholarship on the topic, begins as the symbol of the free poetic word, evolving over time into the Sufi symbol of the illuminated spirit (Nurbakhsh, Vol. IV, 146). In the first verse the notion of the freedom of the spirit becomes tied directly to that of the word (palavra). This union of spirit and word is relatively common in Pessoa's third stage work, as well as is more traditional works of Sufi inspiration [such as that of Ibn Árabi's *Interpreter of Desires* (Simon, *Understanding*, 82)]. It serves to empower the poetic word, i.e., poetic language, in a way that more deconstructive foci would neither endorse nor permit. In fact, it is the speaking of the name that gives the spirit the ability to fly (in symbolic terms), as we see in the fifth verse. This sound then becomes the "the brushing of wings" of the birds that "build the nest in the foliage of speech / and create deep roots in common words / that common lovers make great / when they speak of love" in the poem's final verses. It is here, then, that we find the crux of the poem's message, the transfer of the poetic word, free from constraints in the mutually beneficial relationship with the spirit (hence, the use of the flying bird as opposed to other possible symbols), to the lovers. Again, and as seen in previous scholarship on the topic, the poetic word becomes free in Pessoa's second stage through the Sufi act of mystical union between the lovers. The system set here, then, has a strong precedent in works such as *Os Olhos de Isa* and the continued contradiction of literary postmodernism's essential place in the contemporary mind.

Another important notion expressed here is that of the construction of the nest. This nest is reminiscent of the mystical "house" that the poetic subject constructs as the place for mystical illumination (i.e., the Sufi "qalb") in the work of António Ramos Rosa (Simon, "Mysticism," 58). The speech act, thus, is not only one of mystical empowerment, but of the empowerment to love without limitations. The freedom associated with this type of open, spiritual closeness finds its roots in Pessoa's first stage work, in which his greatest preoccupation consisted of the notions of liberty and the cultural censorship that Pessoa felt existed at that time.

To summarize, while Janés' combination of the mystical and post-modern serves to combat the male hegemony, Pessoa's does so to combat both social and intimate crises (depending on the time period). In both poetries we also see a desire to reach some greater, essential meaning within a deconstructive and de-essentialized context. This contrast to what we find in the works of both Rossetti and Gopegui, in which the mere notion of the essential, universal center is made fodder for the de-constructionist tendencies of the period. Once more, this desire, through this combination of mystical illumination and the analytical process of literary postmodernism's deconstruction, unites in intent and excises it-self in practice of the Portuguese Experimentalists to read the essential which exists beyond the surface of Surrealist or other imageries. In other words, while the purpose of Janés' and Pessoa's work is to attain some type of divine illumination, the application of deconstructive techniques leaves the possibility an inherent contradiction of the process.

Thus, in terms of a shift into the Postmodern paradigm, these poets leave us in a quandary. If Easthope is correct and the adoption phase of a new paradigm will have occurred according to Kuhn's theory, we cannot say then that Janés nor Pessoa's poetries reflect that. Their poetries seem to adhere to mystical and essentialist traditions which still exist in modern Iberian societies while also moving away from the less desirable aspects of those traditions, such as the male-dominated social hegemony of Spain and the dictatorial traditions of Portugal. This means that, if we take these poets' works as an indicator of the peninsula's social climate during the last gasps of the Twentieth Century (an argument for which the processes described at the beginning of this chapter would lend particular credence), a Postmodern paradigm cannot have been adopted in the social or political strata at the point in history. Although it is evident that this paradigm is an extremely strong one, and may eventually take hold entirely in Spanish and Portuguese societies, there remains a counter-current, visible yet decentralized in Rossetti's poetry, while still explicitly active and fundamentally essentialist in the poetry of Janés and Pessoa.

# Conclusions

To conclude this study, I would like to review quickly the principle characteristics of each writer studied. I will then take a minute to describe how each fit into the social and political parameters which, in conjunction, reflect the Paradigm Shift as it takes place in Iberia in the second half of the Twentieth Century. Finally, we will discuss the possibilities for a dominant Postmodern paradigm in the peninsular countries.

The writers of the 1950s in Iberia, as we have seen, seemed on the surface to continue the divergence already existing between the social and experimental trajectories begun in the 1930s in both Spanish and Portuguese literatures. However, it became evident that poets such as González and Rosa, whose works reflected a social preoccupation, also tended to absorb the influence of the intimate poetry of Hierro and Helder, more concerned with capturing the semantic plurality of the signifier than of ignoring it in favor of topics such as social injustice. By the fall of the dictatorships, the social and experimental poetries had united with the external influence of literary postmodernism to form uniquely Iberian strains of the movement. This can be seen first in the polissemic works of Ruy Belo and Moura in Portugal's "revivalist" state; and in Rossetti's poetic of dissonance between the (neo-)classical and deconstructive. So, it seems by the 1980s that, at least in the literary sense, postmodernism has taken hold. Nonetheless, by the end of the Twentieth Century we also see a counter current which rather ironically combines with the postmodern anti-hegemonic, deconstructive tendency in the poetry of Clara Janés and Joaquim Pessoa. It is at this point that we may observe a sort of unification of the two distinctive trajectories, Spanish and Portuguese, melding through the thematic rebellion against the purely denaturalizing effects of postmodernism. As we have also discussed, in the social strata of both Spain and Portugal it is difficult to envision an entirely non-traditional society in either country. As each struggles to maintain a foothold in the present, they also struggle to keep the past from being decentralized out of existence.

It will also be useful to review now the three stages, or phases, of the Paradigm Shift according to Kuhn. The first, or Crisis Phase, is the phase in which the existing paradigm (in this case the Modern paradigm) is no longer able to function as the ruling set of concepts and ideas in a given context. In this case, that context is the dictatorial and post-dictatorial period in Spain and Portugal from approx. 1950 to 1974-5, then to 2000. The second, or Transitional Phase, of the Paradigm Shift occurs when several competing paradigms, including versions of the defunct paradigm, begin to vie for dominance. We see this in the social, and thus poetic, landscape of the 1950s and 60s. As the dictatorships must modify their policies and practices, collapsing later on (through evidently differing processes), and the social stratification which has ruled the peninsula begins to break down, poetic tendencies reflect the process through the various competing, then merging, social and intimate poetries that appear. Finally, the Adoption Phase signals the return of some sort of stability, as one of the competing paradigms becomes dominant.

Thus, while we may argue that a Paradigm Shift has occurred, we cannot state that it is entirely completed. The Postmodern paradigm, or the unified social Postmodernity and literary postmodernism as a set of principles governed through the notions of deconstruction and decentralization, has evidently become the primary set of concepts governing most aspects of life and art in the Iberian Peninsula. The issue of whether or not a paradigm shift has occurred is not a closed one, however. The ambiguity present in Hierro's and González's work is not necessarily new, but rather also present in the poetry of earlier Twentieth-Century poets such as Lorca and Salinas. Also, in all the above writers there is an appreciation for the presence of older forms, such as the presence of Golden Age themes and characters in Rossetti's poetry. Finally, all essentialist poetry has not vanished, as work by poets such as Clara Janés (who is noted for both her anti-phallocentrism as well as her use of Christian, Zoroastrian and Sufi mystical symbolism) and Joaquim Pessoa demonstrate. Thus, it is possible that peninsular poetry, and thus peninsular culture, could be in the throes of a Transitional Phase whose final paradigm choice may be as surprising as it will be necessary.

To summarize, in terms of the feasibility of an argument in favor of a complete paradigm shift having already been reflected in Iberian poetic art, it is difficult to assume that this has happened yet. It would occur to anyone who has studied the sweeping thematic and technical changes of Spanish and Portuguese poetry from the 1950s through the beginning of the 21st Century, however, that some sort of change is definitely afoot.

As the techniques of testimonial, intimate, experimental and postmodern poetics emerged in these two countries, there remained a consistent counter-balance. This included the revalorization of Iberian Renaissance and Baroque Period poetries (such as those of Camões or Quevedo) and the presence and influence of the Christian, Kabbalic and Sufi mystical processes in several poetic works of the period. There is one other possibility, however, which we will discuss in the Appendix.

# Appendix

In the 21st Century the poetic landscape has exploded in a plethora of ways. First, the introduction to internet blogs and on-line publishing has given Spanish and Portuguese poets of all types (and, I must say, talents) a venue for their work's dissemination.[15] Second, the resurgence of poetry as what one could call a "sellable media," meaning that it has become a secondary marketable good, has given older poets and their work a chance for a re-reading. Yet, we tend to find poets drawn to older forms, even when the themes of their poems reflect yet newer realities facing them (terrorism, the new global economy, etc). Thus, poetry has grown as a form of popular culture while simultaneously maintaining its image as a more haughty literary style (this in comparison to the novel, which has taken the primary role in mass-published works in the 21st Century).

To this Iberian poetic manifestation we may assign an adherence to traditional poetic forms, topics and cultural limits, even given the extension to which the new forms of electronic publishing make a world-wide readership possible. Despite this, the combination of a deconstructive discourse, and vivid and ironic anachronisms, such as Pessoa's mystical deconstruction, and the presence of kitsch imagery, such as that found in Rossetti's work, bring literary postmodernism within the auspices of this new poetic tradition.

I would like to suggest, then, that the peninsular cultures may be closer to the 3rd· or adoption, phase of a Postmodern paradigm, than previously thought. Again, the Adoption Phase of Kuhn's Theory of the Paradigm Shift states that the community accepts one as the dominant paradigm (Dietze 39). As we have seen time and time again, there seems to be a uniqueness to Iberian Postmodernity, Iberian literary postmodernism and, hence, our Postmodern paradigm. This is one which incorpo-

---

15. Carmelo discussed this new poetic venue in *A Novíssima Poesia Portuguesa e a Experiência Estética*. Mem Martins: Publicações Europa-América, 2005.

rates both the deconstructive, decentralizing, denaturalizing and egalitarian forces which define the postmodern, while also revitalizing the older Iberian traditions as both joined and countering the postmodern tendency. However contradictory this situation may seem, it also makes perfect sense considering the status of Spain and Portugal in today's larger world, two countries made up of several nations, cultures and problematic social conditions.

So, while we may conclude that the Postmodern paradigm is dominant, we must do what others have done in the past. That is to say, the paradigm cannot be called "Postmodern," as the term is too strict in its definition to encompass all that is Iberia. Rather, we may call it the "Iberian Postmodern paradigm," one whose forces and counter-forces take into account all of the conflicting sentiments and guiding notions of these colonizers turned intra-European colonies.

We may then begin to define an "Iberian Postmodern paradigm" as both deconstructive and traditional, mystical yet wary of the Modern paradigm's tendency toward essentialism. It has revitalized the genre of poetry in the peninsula, giving it the ability to express all of the nuances of Spanish and Portuguese cultures as they have developed over the past thirty years, divided yet somehow complementary, and constantly evolving toward understanding of themselves and an acceptance of each other (as in the case of Janés' translations of António Ramos Rosa) in their perpetual cultural and literary polissemy.

As I stated in this study's introduction, nonetheless, we should use caution when approaching such topics in that, through our own desire as literary critics to categorize and define, we do not overly simplify such complex processes as those analyzed here. I leave it, then, to a future study to decide whether or not the title of "Iberian" should be placed on this (or any other) genre or paradigm, or if it is enough to say that the Iberian countries have found themselves in what we may consider to be a "late Transitional Phase." If Ruy Belo is right in saying that poetry "communicates" the will of the people (Belo, *País*, 8), then it will continue to indicate to us in the near future exactly what to make of the fascinating evolution of the Iberian societies.

# Bibliography

Álvares, Cláudia. "On *White Mythologies*: Detotalising the Legacy of Modernity." *Culture, Theory and Critique*. 46.2 (2005): 93-113

Andrade, Eugénio de. "Nota sobre Vasco Graça Moura." *Letras e Letras*. 7.110 (July 1994): 43.

Baradez, François:

――――. "A Arte Vinga a Vida." *Letras e Letras*. 7.110 (1994 July): 39-40.

――――. "Naufrágio de Sepúlveda: «Um Estili Brilhante»." *Letras e Letras*. 7.110 (July 1994): 38.

Barthes, Roland. *Mythologies*. 2nd Edition, Translated by Annette Lavers. New York: Hill and Wang, 1972.

Belo, Ruy.

――――. *Obra Poética de Ruy Belo*. Vol. 1. Organized by Joaquim Manuel Magalhães. Lisboa: Editorial Presença, 1981.

――――. *País Possível*. Lisboa: Assírio e Alvim, 1973.

Blanco, José. "Vida e Transfiguração: Brevíssima Nota a Propósito (de uma Parte) de Último Livro de Versos de Vasco Graça Moura." *Letras e Letras*. 7.110 (July 1994): 41-42.

Bleich, David. "The Subjective Paradigm in Science, Psychology, and Criticism." *New Literary History*. 7.2 (1976 Winter): 313-334.

Bloom, Lynn Z.; Daiker, Donald A.; White, Edward M.; Eds. *Composition Studies in the New Millennium: Rereading the Past, Rewriting the Future*. Carbondale, IL: Southern Illinois University Press, 2003.

Boggs, Bruce A. "Music, Metaphor and Emotion in the Poetry of José Hierro." *Hispania*. 86.2 (2003 May): 209-219.

Bou, Enric and Soria Olmedo, Andrés. "Postmodernity and Literature in Spain." *International Postmodernism: Theory and Literary Practice*. Ed. Hans Bertens and Douwe Fokkema. Amsterdam: John Benjamins Publishing Company, 1997. 397-403.

Branco, Cristina. *Sensus*. Universal, 2001.

Camões, Luís Vaz de. *Os Lusíadas*. Emanuel Paulo Ramos, Ed. Porto: Porto Editora, 2000.

Carmelo, Luís. *A Novíssima Poesia Portuguesa e a Experiência Estética*. Mem Martins: Publicações Europa-América, 2005.

Chillida, Eduardo. http://www.eduardo-chillida.com/

Cilveti, Ángel L. *La Literatura mística española:Antología I. La Edad Media.* Madrid: Taurus Ediciones, 1983.

Crow, John. *Spain: The Root and the Flower.* Berkeley, CA: University of California Press, 1985.

Culler, Jonathan:

————. *On Deconstruction.* Ithaca, NY: Cornell University Press; 1982.

————. "At the Boundaries: Barthes and Derrida." *At the Boundaries: Proceedings of the Northeastern University Center for Literary Studies.* Vol I. Ed. Herbert L Sussman. Boston: Northeastern University Press, 1983. 23-40.

Dal Farra, Maria Lúcia. "Vôo de Teto-Teto: Sobre a Poesia de Herberto Helder." *Estudos Portugueses e Africanos.* (Campinas) 31 (1998 January/June): 17-22.

Debicki, Andrew. *Spanish Poetry of the Twentieth Century: Modernity and Beyond.* Lexington, KY: The University Press of Kentucky, 1994.

Derrida, Jacques. *Positions.* 2nd Edition, Translated and Annotated by Alan Blas. Chicago, IL: The University of Chicago Press, 1981.

Deters, Joseph. "El Desafío de la verdad en la poesía de Ángel González." *Hispanic Journal.* 20.2 (1999 Fall): 239-247.

Dietze, Erich von. *Paradigms Explained: Rethinking Thomas Kuhn's Philosophy of Science.* Westport, CT: Praeger Press, 2001.

Easthope, Anthony. "Paradigm Lost and Paradigm Regained." *The State of Theory.* Richard Bradford, Ed. London: Routledge, 1993. 90-104.

Ferradáns, Carmela. "La Seducción de la mirada: Manuel Vázquez Montalbán y Ana Rossetti.' *Revista Canadiense de Estudios Hispánicos.* 22.1 (1997 Fall): 19-31.

Ferreira, Agostino de Jesus Ribeiro. "Rejeição e Religião em *Os Passos em Volta* de Herberto Helder." *Brotéria.* 1996: 169-187.

Fisher, Diane. "Montage as Postmodern Ironic Technique in Two Poems from *Procedimientos narrativos* by Ángel González." *Letras Peninsulares.* 9.2-3 (1996-1997): 277-307.

Francis, Natalia. *Resurrección y Metamorfosis hacia un ser d/escrito en amor: la obra de Clara Janés.* Ann Arbor, MI: Dissertation Information Services, 1998.

Frank, Manfred. "Identity and Subjectivity." *Deconstructive Subjectvities.* Ed. Simon Critchley and Peter Dews. New York: State University of New York, 1996. 127-148.

González, Ángel:

————. *Otoños y otras luces.* Barcelona: Tusquets Ediciones, 2001.

————. *101 + 19 = 120 poemas.* 2nd Edition. Prologue by Luis García Montero. Madrid: Visor, 2001.

Gopégui, Belén. *La Escala de los mapas.* 1ª Edición. Barcelona: Editorial Anagrama, S.A., 2003.

Grady, Hugh, ed. *Shakespeare and Modernity: Early Modern to Millenium.* London: Routledge, 2000.

Guimarães, Fernando:

———. *A Poesia da Presença e o Aparecimento do Neo-Realismo.* Porto: Brasília Editora, 1981

———. *A Poesia Contemporânea Portuguesa.* Vila Nova da Famalicão: Quasi Edições, 2002

Gusmão, Manuel. "Notes for a Cartography of Twentieth-Century Portuguese Poetry." *A Revisionary History of Portuguese Literature.* New York: Garland Publishing, Inc., 1999. 153-175.

Harvey, Irene. *Labyrinths of Exemplarity: At the Limits of Deconstruction.* Albany, NY: State University of New York Press, 2002.

Helder, Herberto. *Poesia Toda.* Lisbon: Assírio e Alvim, 1981.

Holloway, Vance. *El Posmodernismo y otras tendencias de la novela española, (1967-1995).* Madrid: Editorial Fundamentos, 1999.

Hooper, John. *The New Spaniards.* 3rd Edition. London: Penguin Books, 1995.

Hutcheon, Linda. *A Poetics of Postmodernism.* New York: Rutledge, 1988.

Hierro, José. *Cuánto sé de mí.* 2nd Edition. Madrid: Ediciones La Palma, 1999.

Iarocci, Michael. *Properties of Modernity: Romantic Spain, Modern Europe, and the Legacies of Empire.* Nashville, TN: Vanderbilt University Press, 2006.

Janés, Clara:

———. *Vivir.* Madrid: Ediciones Hiperión, S. L., 1983.

———. *Creciente Fértil.* Madrid: Ediciones Hiperión, S. L., 1989.

———. *Diván y el ópalo de fuego.* Introduction by Dr. Luce López-Baralt. Murcia: Consejería de Cultura y Educación, 1996.

———. *Arcángel de sombra.* Madrid: Visor Libros, 1999.

Kaufman, Helena and Klobucka, Anna. "Politics and Culture in Postrevolutionary Portugal." in *After the Revolution: twenty years of Portuguese Literature.* Helena Kaufman and Anna Klobucka, Ed. London: Associated University Press, 1997.

Kaup, Monika. "The Future is Entirely Fabulous: The Baroque Genealogy of Latin America's Modernity." *Modern Language Quarterly.* 68.2 (2007 June): 221-41.

Kristeva, Julia. *The Portable Kristeva.* Ed. Kelly Oliver. New York: Columbia University Press, 1997.

Kruger-Robbins, Jill. "Poetry and Film in Postmodern Spain: The Case of Pedro Almodóvar and Ana Rossetti." *Anales de la Literatura Española Contemporánea.* 22.1 (1997): 7-8, 165-179.

Kuhn, Thomas. *The Structure of Scientific Revolutions.* 2nd Edition. Chicago: The University of Chicago Press, 1970.

Ladner, Erik. "The Limits of *Posibilismo*: The Censors and Antonio Buero Vallejo." Diss. U of Texas at Austin, 2006.

Lafollette, Martha. "Writing the Book of Life: Ana Rossetti's *Punto umbrío*." Sherno, Sylvia and West-Settle, Cecile, Ed. *Contemporary Spanish Poetry: The Word and the World*. Madison: Fairleigh Dickinson Unversity Press, 2005.

Lancastre, Maria José de. "Uma das Vozes mais Inovadoras da Melhor Poesia Portuguesa." *Letras e Letras*. 7.110 (1994 July): 36-37.

Legido-Quigley, Eva. "Belén Gopegui." *Twentieth Century Spanish Fiction Writers*. Altisent, Marta E. (ed. and introd.); Martínez-Carazo, Cristina (ed. and introd.). Detroit, MI: Gale, 2006.

Letria, José Jorge. "Joaquim Pessoa: a poesia anunciada." *Jornal de Letras, Artes e Ideias*. 10.442 (1990 December 24-31): 6-7.

Llorente Torres, Marina. *Palabra y deseo: Espacios transgresores en la poesía española, 1975-2000*. Málaga: Universidad de Málaga, 2000.

Longhurst, C.A. "Coming from the Cold: Spain, Modernism and the Novel." *Bulletin of Spanish Studies*. LXXIX(2002): 263-283

López III, Fred A. "Bourgeois State and the Rise of Social Democracy in Spain." in *Transitions from Dictatorship to Democracy: Comparative Studies of Spain, Portugal and Greece*. Chilcote, Ronald et al, Ed. New York: Taylor and Francis, 1990. 17-72.

López-Baralt, Luce:

————. *San Juan de la Cruz y el Islam*. México, D. F.: El Colegio de México, A. C., 1985.

————. "José Hierro ante el milagro más grande del amor: la transformación de la amada en el amado." *La Torre: Revista de la Universidad de Puerto Rico*. 6.21 (1992 Jan-Mar):105-164.

Magalhães, Fernando. *A Poesia Contemporânea Portuguesa*. Lisboa: Edições Quasi, 2002.

Marinho, Maria de Fátima:

————. "O Surrealismo ou o Poder das Imagens." *Letras e Letras*. 36 (1990 December 5): 5-6.

————. "Poesia Portuguesa 1960-1990: A Experiência dos Limites." *Iberoromania*. 34 (1991): 41-54.

Martínez de Soria, A. Bernal. "Humanismo del diecisiete en la postmodernidad del veintiuno." *Studies in Philosophy and Education*. 25 (2006): 47–60

Marson, Ellen Engelson. "Clara Janés: Mysticism and the Search for the Female Poetic Voice." *Revista de Estudios Hispánicos*. 29.2 (1995 May): 245-257.

Martinho, Fernando J. B. "Visões do Fim na Poesia Portuguesa Mais Recente." *Rassegua Iberística*. 62(1998 February): 13-25.

Matos, Joaquim:

————. "Comunicação Académica de Herberto Helder." *Letras e Letras*. 51(1991 July): 11-12.

————. "Uma Palavra Necessária." *Letras e Letras*. 7.110 (1994 July): 45.

Mendes, Ana Paula Coutinho, ed. *O Poeta na Rua: Antologia Portátil de António Ramos Rosa*. Vila Nova da Famalicão: Quasi Edições, 2004.

Miller, Martha LaFollette. "Childhood, Gender, and Religion in the Poetry of Claudio Rodríguez: A Dialogic Response to Frrancoist Discourse." *Hispania.* 91.2 (May 2008): 342-351.

Moura, Vasco Graça. *Letras do Fado Vulgar.* Lisboa: Quetzal Editores, 2001.

Mujica Pinilla, Ramón. *El Collar de la paloma del alma: Amor sagrado y amor profano en la enseñanza de Ibn Hazm y de Ibn 'Arabi.* Prologue by Víctor Danner. Madrid: Hiperión, 1990.

Nataf, Daniel and Sammis, Elizabeth. "Classes, Hegemony and Portuguese Democratization." in *Transitions from Dictatorship to Democracy: Comparative Studies of Spain, Portugal and Greece.* Chilcote, Ronald et al, Ed. New York: Taylor and Francis, 1990. 73-130.

Navarro, António Rebordão. "Para a «Celebração de Modo Mudando." *Letras e Letras.* 7.110 (1994 July): 43.

Newton, Candelas. "Mitopoesis, revisión y delirio en *Creciente Fértil*, de Clara Janés." *Revista Canadiense de Estudios Hispánicos.* 19.1 (1994 Autumn): 109-120.

Nurbakhsh, Javad. *Sufi Symbolism: The Nurbakhsh Encyclopedia of Sufi Terminology.* Vol IV and IX. London: Khaniquahi-Nimatullahi Publications, 1995.

Oliveira, Anabela Diniz Branco de, et al:

———. "Biobibliografia." *Letras e Letras.* 7.110 (1994 July): 32.

———. "Quatro Últimas Canções: O Universo das Casas Labirínticas." *Letras e Letras.* 7.110 (1994 July): 48-50.

———. "Vasco Graça Moura entre os Rostos dos Outros." *Letras e Letras, Letras e Letras.* 7.110 (1994 July): 44-45.

Orringer, Nelson R. "Introduction to Hispanic Modernism." *Bulletin of Spanish Studies.* LXXIX (2002): 133-148.

Pereiro, Peregrina. *La Novela española de los noventa: alternatives éticas a la postmodernidad.* Madrid: Editorial Pliegos, 2002.

Pérez, Janet. "Clara Janés." *Twentieth-Century Spanish Poets.* Jerry Phillips Winfield, Editor. Detroit: Gale Research, Inc., 1993.

Perkins, Juliet. *The Feminine in the Poetry of Herberto Helder.* London: Temesis Books Ltd, 1991.

Pessoa, Joaquim:

———. *O Livro da Noite.* Lisbon: Moraes Editora, 1982.

———. *O Amor Infinito.* Introduction by Roxana Eminescu. Lisbon: Moraes Editora, 1983.

———. *À Mesa do Amor.* Porto: Litexa Editora, 1994.

———. *Obra Poética.* Vol. 1-3. Porto: Litexa Editora, 2001.

———. *Vou-me Embora de Mim.* Porto: Litexa Editora, 2002.

Pinedo, Javier. "José Ortega y Gasset, España y la modernidad." *Cuadernos americanos.* 121 (2007): 41-54.

Pitta, Eduardo. "Os Livros da Margem." *Colóquio/Letras*. 129-130(1993 July-December): 203-205.

Pritchett, Kay, ed. *Four Postmodern Poets of Spain: A Critical Introduction with Translations of the Poems*. Fayetteville: University of Arkansas Press, 1991.

Quadros, António. *A Ideia de Portugal na Literatura Portuguesa dos Últimos 100 Anos*. Lisboa: Fundação Lusíada, 1989.

Rosa, António Ramos:

———. *Gravitações*. Porto: Litexa Editora; 1983.

———. *O Aprendiz Secreto*. Translated by Clara Janés. Madrid: Visor; 2001.

———. *As Palavras*. Porto: Campo Das Letras; 2001.

Rossetti, Ana. *Indicios Vehementes*. With an Interview / Prologue by Jesús Fernández Palacios. Madrid: Ediciones Hiparión, 1985.

Ruiz Soriano, Francisco. "La Cabeza de la percepción y el conocimiento de José Hierro." *Hispania*. 84.1 (2001 March): 20-30.

Sabine, Mark J. L. "'Once but no Longer the Prow of Europe'": National Identity and Portuguese Destiny in José Saramago's *The Stone Raft*. *Portuguese Literary and Cultural Studies*. 6 (2001 Spring): 185-203.

Santos, Boaventura de Sousa. *Pela Mão de Alice: O Social e o Político na Pós-Modernidade*. Porto: Edições Afrontamento, 1994.

Sapelli, Giulio. *Southern Europe since 1945: Tradition and Modernity in Portugal, Spain, Italy, Greece and Turkey*. London: Longman, 1995.

Seixo, Maria-Alzira:

———. "Quatro Últimas Canções: Estreia de Vasco Graça Moura na Ficção." *Letras e Letras*. 7.110 (1994 July): 46-48.

———. "Postmodernism in Portugal." *International Postmodernism: Theory and Literary Practice*. Ed. Hans Bertens and Douwe Fokkema. Amsterdam: John Benjamins Publishing Company, 1997. 405-410.

Simões, Manuel G. "A Errância na Literatura Portuguesa do Século XX." *Rassegua Iberística*. 62 (1998 February): 3-11.

Simon, Robert.

———. *Understanding the Portuguese Poet Joaquim Pessoa: A Study in Iberian Cultural Hybridity*. New York: The Edwin Mellen Press, 2008.

———. "The Paradigm Shift and the Evolution toward Postmodernism in Contemporary Spanish Poetry." *The South Carolina Modern Language Review*, 7.1 (2008). Web.

———. "Mysticism Without Borders: A Comparative Study of Mystical Symbolism in António Ramos Rosa's *O Aprendiz Secreto* and the poetry of Clara Janés." *Ellipsis*. 5 (2007). 41-66.

———. "Não é Apenas a Libertação: A Presença Surrealista e A Desconstrução Pós-moderna na Obra Poética de Herberto Helder." *Portuguese Studies Review*. 16.2 (2009). 147-159.

————. "A Desconstrução da Hegemonia Cristã em *Os Olhos de Isa* de Joaquim Pessoa." *Encruzilhadas/Crossroads.* 7 (2006): 164-174.

Ugalde, Sharon Keefe:

————. *Conversaciones y poemas: la nueva poesía femenina española en castellano.* Siglo Veintiuno Editores: Madrid, 1991.

————. "La Subjetividad desde "lo otro" en la poesía de María Sanz, Victoria Atencia y Clara Janés." *Actos del X Congreso de la Asociación de Hispanistas.* Barcelona, Promociones y Publicaciones Universitarias; 1992. 307-315

————. "Huellas de mujer en la poesía de Clara Janés." *Anales de la Literatura Española Contemporánea.* 18.1 (1993): 193-209.

White, Landeg (trans). *The Lusiads.* Luís Vaz de Camões, author. New York: Oxford World's Classics, USA, 2001.

Wilcox, John C:

————. "Clara Janés: hacia su poemario de los años ochenta." *Actos del X Congreso de la Asociación de Hispanistas.* Barcelona, Promociones y Publicaciones Universitarias, 1992. 353-361.

————. "Ángel González's Intertextualization of Juan Ramón Jiménez." *The Discovery of Poetry: Essays in Honor of Andrew Debicki.* Roberta Johnson, Editor. Boulder: Society of Spanish and Spanish American Studies, 2003.

Universal. *Breve História da Literatura Portuguesa, Autores: Vida e Obra.* Lisboa: Texto Editora, 1999.

# Index

# About the Author

Dr. Robert Simon instructs Spanish and Portuguese Languages, Cultures, and Literatures at Kennesaw State University in Kennesaw, GA. His current publications include a critical book titled *Understanding the Portuguese Poet Joaquim Pessoa: A Study in Iberian Cultural Hybridity* (2008) and various critical studies, as well as several books of poetry including: *The Traveler / el viajero / o Viajante* (2010), *Não Tirei Fotos* (2009), *Os Sophíadas* (2009), and *New Poems from the Airplane and Graveyard* (2007). He, his wife, and daughter live in Georgia.

# Notes

1. Although several articles exist which mention the idea of a Paradigm Shift (such as Colin Richmond's 2008 study, "Malory and Modernity: A Qualm about Paradigm Shifts"), only one, that of Easthope, applies the theory in a concise and systematic manner. It is due to this unique characteristic that I have chosen to focus on this particular article as a basis for utilizing Kuhn's theory in a literary and cultural context.

2. I have chosen to forgo an analysis of the "novísimos," a group of essentially pre-postmodern poets in Spain, as part of this study. This is both for the sake of brevity, as well as due to the presence here of sufficient examples of both social and intimate tendencies in Spanish / Iberian poetics so as to make clear the point of the competing voices of each tendency. I do, however, mention them briefly in Chapter II.